Troublesome Business

Geoffrey Bell

Troublesome Business

The Labour Party and the
Irish Question

First published by Pluto Press Limited,
Unit 10 Spencer Court, 7 Chalcot Road, London NW1 8LH

British Library Cataloguing in Publication Data
Bell, Geoffrey
    Troublesome Business: the Labour Party and the Irish
    Question.
    1. Labour Party (*Great Britain*)   2. Ireland — Politics
    and government — 19th century
    3. Ireland — Politics and government — 20th century
    I. Title
    941.5082   DA959

    ISBN 0-86104-373-1

Cover illustration by John Minnion
Cover design by Michael Mayhew

Typeset by Grassroots Typeset, London NW6
Printed in Great Britain by Photobooks (Bristol) Ltd,
Barton Manor, St Philips, Bristol BS2 0RN

Contents

Acknowledgements

Many people have helped me in many different ways in writing this book. I would give special mention to Pete Ayrton, Stephen Bird, Paddy Byrne, Reg Freeson, Mary Margaret McHugh, Kevin McNamara and Jock Stallard.

Extra thanks to James McBeigh, who helped with research into the Campaign of Democracy in Ulster.

I also acknowledge Barry Stubbs, whose thesis on aspects of the British Labour Party and Ireland I discovered rather late in my research, but which guided me to sources I had missed. Thanks also to those who work at the library of the London School of Economics, the Labour Party Library, the British Museum Newspaper Library, the Public Record Office and the Belfast Public Record Office.

Introduction

This is the first published detailed account of the history of the British Labour Party's policy on the Irish national question.

This is not to make an extravagant claim of originality, but it is difficult to understand why the topic has been neglected. The failure to produce such a history suggests a theoretical apathy which may explain much of the failures of British socialism.

It is a record rather than an interpretation and, hopefully, others will correct and expand this work.

Shortly before the 1916 Easter Rising the revolutionary socialist James Connolly met the socialist pacifist Francis Sheehy-Skeffington and his equally political wife, Hanna. Connolly and Francis were soon to be killed.

Hanna had always wondered about Connolly's real view on religion and knowing the Rising was imminent decided to make one last probe into his faith, or lack of it.

'Tell me, Jim, do you think there will be anything on the other side?'

'The British Labour Party?' said Connolly. 'They won't lift a finger to help us!'

1. The Inheritance

A century ago, two Irish politicians argued whether British socialists and the British working class had an affinity with the cause of Irish freedom. One was Charles Parnell, leader of the Irish Home Rule Party, a Protestant, a landlord and a politician of shrewd craft and daring originality. The other was Michael Davitt, one-time member of the insurrectionary Fenian Brotherhood, leader of Ireland's landless peasants, a radical and romantic.

Davitt believed: 'The rising democracy of England are not animated with feelings of hatred towards the people of Ireland. I believe, on the contrary, they are willing that Ireland should have those rights, political and social that they themselves are demanding.'[1]

Parnell was sceptical of such visions. He expressed the view: 'We are told of some great wave of English democracy which is coming over here to poor Ireland to assist the Irish democracy. The poor Irish democracy will have, I fear, to rely upon themselves in the future as they have had up to the present.'[2]

At the time the argument seemed academic. In 1885, the year after Parnell wrote those words, he had secured for the cause of Irish Home Rule the support of William Gladstone and his mighty party. With the Liberals committed to the solving of the Irish question on terms which the Irish themselves had demanded, the ending of the ancient British/Irish conflict appeared only a matter of months, or at the most a couple of years away. What then did it matter whether Davitt's friends in the tiny socialist groups in Britain felt of the same mind, for what power did they possess to influence the great affairs of state? The issue would surely have long been settled by the time the embryonic party of the British working class had attained full maturity.

Irish history is littered with such dashed hopes. Within a few years of Parnell dismissing the potential of the 'English democracy' coming to Ireland's aid, he was dead, the party he had led was divided, the Liberals had split over the Irish issue and the Conservative Party was embarking on a long period of virtually uninterrupted rule. Consequently, the accuracy of Davitt's judgement as to the solidarity the common people of England felt towards the aspirations of the common people of Ireland was to have a relevance which he could not have imagined.

It may be useful to begin this study with an examination of Davitt's belief in the decade he expressed it and in the one that followed. For, although it would be a few years before the British Labour Party was finally established, the preceding years inform much of what was to follow.

So what exactly was this rising democracy of which Davitt spoke?

At the time of Gladstone's conversion to Irish Home Rule, the working class and socialist movements in Britain were politically fragile and quantatively puny. In the mid-1880s, of those organisations with even the slightest national significance, the Social Democratic Federation had no more than a thousand members, the Socialist League had less than half that and the Fabian Society contained no more than 150 adherents.[3] There was no independent working class representation in parliament — the leaders of the growing trade-union movement were content to rely on the Liberals.

However, where there was even a hint of life there was hope and, as to the Irish cause of self-government, some substance, as far as one of the organisations was concerned.

The Social Democratic Federation leader was Henry Meyers Hyndman, an intransigent opponent of the capitalist system who, pending what he believed was its inevitable collapse, played its stock market. An arrogant individual, Hyndman shared a good deal of the prejudices of the upper class into which he had been born, in particular strong anti-German and anti-Jewish sentiments. Yet on Ireland he was not chauvinist. Indeed, the Democratic Federation which he helped to found in 1881, and which was to evolve into the SDF, was, according to Hyndman, established because of the 'coercion of Ireland'. In 1881, four years before the Liberals' adoption of Home Rule, Hyndman told an interviewer:

What gave impetus to the formation of the Federation, as is at present the principal cause for its existence, was the action of the government in relation to Ireland... [where] the government has launched a war of brutal tyranny such as not even a Tory government could have successfully attempted.[4]

This interview originally appeared in the *Irish World*, so Hyndman might be suspected of playing to the readership of the nationalist newspaper. However, the founding conference of the (S)DF did pledge itself to 'end coercion in Ireland'[5] and much of its early activity was directed to that end.[6] In 1881 Hyndman visited Dublin where he joined the Land League, the revolutionary mass movement of the Irish peasantry which had been organised by Davitt with Parnell as its president. The same year the (S)DF assisted in an election campaign of a Land League candidate in County Tyrone, while Hyndman subsequently served on the Land League of Great Britain, which saw itself as the auxiliary to the Irish movement.

Meetings in Britain on the Irish issue were also organised by the (S)DF, on occasions in conjunction with others. One of these, in St James Hall, London in October 1883, was described by Hyndman as, 'the most distinctly revolutionary gathering that has been held in London for over 35 years'.[7]

Yet 'revolutionary' was not exactly what the bulk of the British working class looked for in a political party in the early 1880s, and Hyndman was to admit that this class generally shared the hostility of others towards the Land League.[8]

With the conversion of Gladstone to Irish Home Rule and the winning by the League of various reforms in the Irish land system, the SDF's championing of the Irish cause lost much of its impetus and distinctiveness. Consequently, in the late 1880s, the SDF directed its agitation elsewhere, particularly towards the unemployed. Nevertheless, right to the end of his life, Hyndman was to hold Davitt in the highest regard. His memoirs in 1912 described the Irishman along with the Italian radical Garibaldi as the two greatest leaders of the nineteenth century. Of Davitt he wrote: 'No nobler character ever fought for the independence and well-being of his country.'[9]

The early activities of the (S)DF provide one clue to the optimism with which Davitt looked upon the help that could be offered to the Irish by the 'English democracy'. That was not the only positive indication. The Socialist League, which split from the SDF in 1884, was short-lived, but contained a number of individuals of some prominence in the early history of the British socialist movement — most notably William Morris, Eleanor Marx and Edward Aveling. They, with Karl Marx himself, stressed 'the necessity', in Eleanor's words, 'of helping poor old Ireland'.[10]

Karl Marx was not short of scientific reasons why Ireland should be an issue for British workers. As early as 1869 he expressed the view:

> I have become more and more convinced — and the only question is to drive this conviction home to the English working class — that it can never do anything decisive here in England until it separates its policy with regard to Ireland most definitely from the policy of the ruling classes, until it not only makes common sense with the Irish but actually takes the initiatives in dissolving the Union, established in 1801, and replacing it by a free federal relationship. And this must be done, not as a matter of sympathy with Ireland but as a demand made in the interests of the English proletariat. If not, the English people will remain tied to the leading strings of the ruling class, because it will have to join with them in a common front against Ireland.[11]

Marx's contentions were based on theoretical arguments which need not be elaborated here, for that would imply, falsely, that marxism had a weighty ideological influence on the formation and growth of the Labour Party. What should be mentioned is that the premises on which Marx and Engels based their opinions were eventually proven questionable. The first was that the English aristocracy had its 'entrenched outposts' in Ireland and if they were overrun by the 'natives' then 'the abolition of the aristocracy (to a large extent the same persons as the English landlords) will be infinitely easier here'.[12]

Second, Marx argued that because the contemporary English workers saw themselves in competition with Irish immigrants in the labour market, they identified with the oppression of Ireland by the English ruling class. 'The attitude' of the English workers towards their Irish counterparts, argued Marx, 'is much the same as the "poor whites" to the "niggers" in the former slave states of the USA... this antagonism is the secret of the impotence of the English working class'.[13]

However sound these judgements may have been at the time they were to be bypassed by events. Although the landlords were to be driven out of Ireland between 1870 and 1903, no similar social revolution occurred in England. Nor can the argument be sustained that divisions between English and Irish workers in Britain are sufficient to explain the non-arrival of the socialist millennium.

The general point Marx was making when framing his arguments may have some validity. Certainly, many have maintained that the identification with the 'national interest' by the British working class has crucially hindered their political development.[14] However, it is a long time since the chief manifestation of that trait has been an anti-Irish sentiment.

Whatever the theoretical failings of Marx and Engels on Ireland, both of them did display an enthusiasm, even at times an infatuation, for the struggle taking place there. Marx called the Irish 'more passionate and revolutionary in character than the English',[15] while Engels once declared: 'Give me 200,000 Irishmen and I could overthrow the entire British monarchy'.[16] And throughout her life Eleanor Marx was active at Irish demonstrations and platforms.

Marx and his comrades can confidently be added to the SDF in the list of those who gave flesh to Michael Davitt's views, expressed in 1880, that: 'The cause of Ireland today is that of humanity and labour throughout the world'.[17] Who else provided grounds for such optimism?

What of the Fabian Society, whose members were to have a more profound effect on the ideology of many future stalwarts of the Labour Party than Karl Marx and his followers? A taste of what the early Fabians thought of Ireland and the Irish is given in a message to the conference of the Independent Labour Party in 1899: 'The Fabian Society has resolved to undertake special propaganda in Ireland. This is a development of socialist missionary work which we feel sure will have important results'.[18]

This socialist equivalent of the white man's burden being carried by imperial Britain to far-flung corners of the world was not untypical of the Fabian Society. Two leading members, Sidney and Beatrice Webb, visited Ireland in 1892 and showed the same colonial mentality. They wrote to a friend in England:

'We will tell you about Ireland when we come back. The people are charming but we detest them, as we should the Hottentots, for their very virtues. Home Rule is an absolute necessity in order to depopulate the country of this detestable race'.[19]

Engels described the Fabians as 'proud of their noble magnanimity with which they, the "educated" bourgeoisie condescend to emancipate the workers'.[20] For the Fabians, socialism was the search for moral self-improvement, the attainment of a higher ethical standard. It was about education and order, to be won by reasoned argument and 'permeation' of the existing institutions by men and women, such as themselves, of high principle. The Fabians had a deep distrust, even loathing of the ordinary masses.

Since their socialism lacked the ideological totality of the marxists in or out of the SDF, it had gaping holes. Issues like the Boer War were avoided. It, insisted Sidney Webb and George Bernard Shaw, 'lay outside the special province of the Society'.[21]

Ireland was another issue they ducked. It was not until 1900 that they published a tract on the Home Rule controversy. It gave substance to Davitt's claim that the Fabians were putting 'political enmity between the labour cause of Great Britain and that of Home Rule'.[22] The tract sought to counterpose Home Rule with strong municipal authorities: 'Very few Irishmen have yet realised that in the year 1898 a change was made in the government of Ireland greater than that made by many famous revolutions... in that year, at one blow, the Local Government Act swept away the old oligarchical authorities'.[23]

This overdramatic interpretation of the benefits of municipal reform was typical. The Fabians generally overestimated the effect and power of local councils and, in the specific Irish context, this fitted a general dismissiveness of the Irish national question. The tract also said:

> The plain reason why Englishmen care so little about the wrongs of Ireland is that they suffer from just about the same wrongs themselves on a much greater scale and often in a crueller form... what the Fabian Society has to say on the Irish Question is exactly what it has to say on the English Question; and that is, that the workers of a nation have no enemies except the idlers of it; that the poor are always oppressed no matter what government they live under; and that nothing will rescue the Irish and English worker except giving

them control through their votes and elected representatives.[24]

The Fabians' argument that the Irish national question had little to do with socialism and that it did a disservice by substituting national boundaries for class lines, was an argument which was to reappear time and again. Although this theory did not originate with the Fabians it is important that they should have accepted it. For, while the significance of the role played by the Society in the formation of the Labour Party should not be overestimated, many of the future leaders of the party did share and were influenced by Fabian ideology, and that ideology is part of the inheritance bequeathed to the modern Labour Party. So it is important to note that, at the end of the last century, while the majority of the Society could be described as un-enthusiastic supporters of Irish Home Rule, their support was not so much for national independence, but stemmed from the more central tenet of the Fabian creed concerning the desirability of decentralised government. This emphasis was shared by many in the contemporary socialist movement. When those who adhered to it advocated Irish Home Rule they often bracketed it with the call for parliaments for Scotland, Wales and England.

The views of the Fabians did not go unchallenged. Their 'socialist missionary work' was criticised by James Connolly who, in 1896, after a political apprenticeship in Scotland, formed the Irish Republican Socialist Party:

> Ireland has not until last year received much attention from the Fabian gentry. The Irish worker had not the municipal franchise, therefore Fabian gas and water schemes would have been lost on him. But as soon as he obtained the franchise and manifested the desire to use it in a true class spirit, the cry went up from the Fabian missionaries. In order to prevent the Irish working class from breaking off entirely from the bourgeois parties and from developing a revolutionary tendency, the Fabians sent their lecturer to Ireland, to induce the Irish working class to confine themselves to the work of municipalising.[25]

The animosity was mutual. A patronising J. Bruce Glasier, the personal embodiment of the Fabian mission, said of Connolly after watching him on a pro-Boer demonstration: 'How I envied his self-indulgence and irresponsibility. How straight and broad, but ah, how exhilarating seemed the path along which he was careering with the policeman at his heels'.[26]

Connolly was a revolutionary, the Fabian's gradualists and reformists. But on Ireland Connolly's differences with them and with many other English socialists were not confined to dealing with the argument that Irish nationalism was a diversion from socialism. There was also the question of how far Irish separation should proceed, whether the Home Rule solution of an Irish parliament subservient to Westminster, as advocated by Parnell and those who followed him in the Irish Parliamentary Party, was sufficient. Or whether, as Connolly and the Irish Republican Socialist Party argued, socialists should be demanding complete Irish independence.

Connolly took up both socialism versus nationalism and Home Rule versus independence arguments in an article in 1898. In reply to 'many English socialists' who said agitation for Irish self-determination was 'mere chauvinism' which 'perpetuates national rivalries and race hatred', Connolly insisted:

> Under a socialist system every nation will be the supreme arbiter of its own destinies, national and international; will be forced into no alliance against its will, but will have its independence guaranteed and its freedom respected by the enlightened self-interest of the socialist democracy of the world.[27]

Connolly went on to indict the 'invincible ignorance and unconquerable national egotism of the British electorate', and to complain that the 'English comrades' were prone to side with 'the Home Ruler' who 'disavows all desire for separation' against 'the Socialist Republican'.

Connolly's point was crucial. In the following two decades the issue of Home Rule versus separation would eventually dominate the debates within the Labour Party.

The optimism with which Michael Davitt viewed the 'English democracy' and its attitude to Ireland was not shared by Connolly writing 15 years later. However, he did have the experience of the Independent Labour Party (ILP) on which to base his judgement.

If any organisation can be described as the forerunner of the Labour Party it is the ILP, founded at a conference in Bradford in 1893. Within a year it had become the largest socialist organisation in Britain. By 1895 it had some 20,000 in its ranks. For Frederick Engels the ILP was a welcome change from the 'sectarian' SDF and the 'careerists' of the Fabian Society.[28] The new organisation was no more marxist than the Fabians, although, unlike the Society, there were marxists within its ranks. What distinguished it, and what explains its relative success, was that it combined much of the Fabians' politics with the SDF's orientation towards the working class.

Right from the start the ILP was overwhelmingly working class. From early on its major tactical approach was to win the trade unions (i.e. the mass organisations of the working class which existed at that time), to the cause of independent labour representation in parliament. Minor electoral success had already been achieved before the ILP was founded, with three independent labour candidates, Keir Hardie, John Burns and Havelock Wilson, winning seats at the 1892 general elections.

That election had provided the opportunity for these and a handful of their similar candidates to say where they stood on the Irish issue. The election campaign largely centred on Gladstone's further attempts to legislate Home Rule, and it is noteworthy that those labour candidates' election addresses of which we have a record all endorse Home Rule: though with different levels of enthusiasm. The Middlesbrough election address of Havelock Wilson saw support for Home Rule heading the list of his policy statements,[29] while Ben Ellis, who stood in Peckham, supported Irish Home Rule in the general context of Home Rule for Ireland, Scotland, England and Wales. Keir Hardie, who stood in West Ham, also called for parliaments for the four counties. His election address claimed: 'Since 1879 I have been an advocate and supporter of the movement to secure Home Rule for Ireland'. But he added the proviso that Home Rule was only permissable 'provided the supremacy of the Imperial parliament be maintained unimpaired'.

All of which suggested a Fabian rather than a Connolly interpretation of Irish self-government. Nevertheless, since some form of commitment to the Irish cause was included in these 1892 addresses, this seemed to augur well for the policy of the foundling ILP the following year. But, although the party was formed when Irish Home Rule was at the centre of the national political stage — with the passing of Gladstone's Home Rule Bill in the Commons and its rejection by the Lords — there was no debate at the ILP founding conference on what policy it should adopt on the Irish question. Nor was any position on Home Rule inserted into the extensive programme agreed at the Bradford conference.

In one sense that was not surprising. The ILP sought to address itself to matters of material concern to the British working class; to social reform, payment of MPs, universal suffrage, the eight-hour working day. Ireland was secondary to such considerations. A solution to the problem appeared imminent, and, anyway, the issue had become the hobby-horse of the Liberals. None of the 'Labour' MPs contributed to the long debates over Gladstone's Home Rule Bill.

It is an interesting contrast that while the Irish question was a stimulus in the formation of the (S)DF in 1881, the only time Ireland was even partially debated at the early conferences of the ILP was during a motion at the 1897 conference which protested the jailing of three anarchists in Britain and added 'also those imprisoned in connection with the Home Rule Movement'.

There was a further passing reference at the 1901 ILP conference when, in his chairman's address, J. Bruce Glasier of Fabian mission fame but also of the ILP, noted, 'The presence of 80 Irish representatives in the House of Commons who were proud to call themselves rebels.'[30]

By the time Glasier made that remark a further decisive step had been taken in the formation of the Labour Party with the establishment, in 1900, of the Labour Representation Committee (LRC). It was to become the Labour Party six years later.

Organisationally, the LRC was a coalition of all that had gone before. The ILP, SDF and Fabians received guaranteed seats on the LRC executive until 1918, although the SDF soon gave up theirs. What was new were the affiliations from the trade unions. They grew rapidly following the Taff Vale legal judgement of 1901 which seriously threatened the right to strike and convinced trade union leaders of the need for their own political voice in parliament. But in securing the participation of the unions, the socialists had to pay a price. The union leaders were generally well to the right of the socialist groups, with most of them, like the early Labour MPs, sanctioning an organisational but not an ideological break from Liberalism. Thus, the founding conference of the LRC heavily defeated a motion calling for 'recognition of the class struggle' and the aim of 'socialisation of the means of production, distribution and exchange', in favour of securing the election to parliament of 'men sympathetic with the aims and demands of the labour movement'.[31]

Such restricted ambitions meant that the broader political issues attracted little interest from the trade union leaders. Right up to the outbreak of the first world war in 1914, the Labour Party's discussions of foreign affairs — and these were judged to include Ireland — were usually left to the members of the socialist societies.[32]

For the Irish and their cause of self-government, this was not a great disadvantage. Since the trade union leaders and several others in the LRC and early Labour Party maintained an identification with the politics of the Liberals, it was inevitable that part of Labour's ideological inheritance would be Liberal policy on Ireland. Indeed, the LRC manifesto for the 1900 general election did call for 'legislative independence for all parts of the Empire'. However, this was not unanimously endorsed in the election addresses of the 15 candidates. Of the 11 which remain in the Labour Party archives, eight voiced some form of support for Irish Home Rule. The other three candidates, Richard Bell, F.W. Jowett and George Lansbury, made no reference to the issue.

Whatever the views of the early pioneers of independent working class representation on the Irish question, there was a further aspect to the relationship between the origins of the Labour Party and Ireland. In a letter written to *The Times* in 1888, H.H. Champion, another early advocate of labour representation in parliament, observed: 'I find that Home Rule is "practical politics" because the Irish vote [in parliament] counts, and that the labour problem is not "practical politics" because the labour vote is not effectively organised'.[33]

The clear implication was that if the Irish could organise separately and get scores of MPs, why should the working class of Britain not follow their example? British socialists posed such rhetorical questions many times up to and after the formation of the LRC. Keir Hardie told the ILP conference of 1901: 'The outstanding feature of this parliament was the way in which it was dominated by the Irish Party'.[34] And to the left of Hardie, Eleanor Marx argued in 1890: 'Why has the Liberal Party been so suddenly converted to Home Rule? Simply because the Irish people sent 80 members to the House of Commons to support the Conservatives: in the same way we must kick these Liberal and Radical members out if they refuse to support our programme'.[35]

Earlier, in 1887, the Labour Electoral Association in a reference to the Irish Parliamentary Party had reasoned: 'Recent events have shown what an active and united party can do in the House of Commons... it has practically succeeded in emancipating a people'.[36]

Consequently, there were parallels between the manner in which the party of Parnell, its successor led by John Redmond, and the Labour Party were organised and tactically conceived. The first manifesto of the LRC declared the organisation was 'fully alive to the fact that the great battles between capital and labour are to be fought out in the division lobbies of the House of Commons',[37] which was an argument against those, such as the SDF, who warned against reliance on the parliamentary method. Similarly, in 1882, when Parnell sought to replace the mass movement of the Land League by the National League, which was no more than an election machine, Davitt complained of the 'complete eclipse by a purely parliamentary substitute of what had been a semi-revolutionary organisation'.[38]

But it was this 'parliamentary substitute' which Labour's pioneers so envied and sought to reproduce. Davitt's constant mistrust of Parnell was not shared by the advocates of the parliamentary tactic within the British socialist movement. On the contrary, Keir Hardie in 1894 described Parnell as 'the one man in politics for whom, as a politician, I was ever to feel genuine respect'.[39]

The impact of the Irish in the House of Commons on Labour's pioneers bears stressing because it is one often overlooked by historians of the British Labour Party. On the other hand it is important to underline the different ways the Irish nationalists and the founders and builders of the Labour Party viewed the House of Commons. Irish nationalists like Parnell worked through parliament but saw its control of everything Irish as a block to reform and progress in Ireland. The Labour pioneers noted what had been achieved by way of social reform and extension of the franchise and concluded parliament was a permanent means to progress.

Those contrasting assessments were to confront each other a number of times in the last 15 years of the century. In doing so, another theme, which was to recur in the succeeding decades, cropped up. To discover what that was it was best to return to Parnell's warning that the Irish national movement should not rely on the good offices of British political parties to win self-government. Parnell had made that statement prior to Gladstone's conversion, after which Parnell tended to tie himself to the Liberals. Again, this was the Irish using the British parliamentary system and the parties which operated within it as a means to an end. However, for Davitt and other Irish radicals who supported both Irish Home Rule and the cause of independent working class representation in parliament, Parnell's alliance with the Liberals posed a dilemma, which first surfaced when Keir Hardie stood in a by-election in Mid-Lanarkshire in April 1888.

Originally, it had seemed Hardie would be adopted as a Liberal candidate. Davitt had canvassed this at the national Liberal headquarters. When the party establishment rejected the suggestion, Hardie stood on an independent ticket as a representative of the 'National Labour Party'. Davitt was faced with a conflict of interest: to back Hardie, whose political philosophy he generally shared; or to support the pro-Home Rule Liberal who stood a better chance of defeating the anti-Home Rule candidates.

Davitt chose Hardie, but the Irish National League, the Catholic Church and Parnell all urged the 1,300 Irish electors in the constituency to vote for the Liberal candidate. One branch of the National League, the 'Home Government branch of Glasgow' did endorse Hardie,[40] but he still came bottom of the poll with 617 votes.

The Irish issue did not lose Hardie the election, but it did pose a new and very real tactical problem for the supporters of both Home Rule and independent labour. Davitt tackled the issue in a private letter:

> It would be better, I admit... not to divide Liberal constituencies now upon the issue of direct parliamentary representation [of labour]... It must be preceded by organisation adequate to

the work of substituting, and paying for, men from the industrial ranks for MPs who belong to the 'upper classes'. But
it is quite another thing to assail English or Scotch working
men with bitter abuse for daring to run an issue of their own
across the path of Home Rule. It will be remembered by
Scotch working men (who were Home Rulers before Gladstone) that Irish MPs were sent from London to oppose the
labour candidate.[41]

Davitt wrestled with this problem for ten years. The 1892
general election was fought specifically on the Home Rule issue
and he decided the priority was to support Liberal candidates.
But this election also marked the beginning of independent
labour representation in parliament — with the victories of Har-
die, Burns and Wilson — so the predicament of Davitt and other
Irish radicals grew more acute. Davitt supported Burns and
Wilson at the polls, but in general he endorsed the Liberal Party.
Consequently, he and Hardie became bitter political enemies.
Davitt wrote: 'I believe Keir Hardie and Co are secret enemies of
the Home Rule cause.'[42] Hardie replied: 'In the readiness of the
Irish to do the dirty scavenging work of the Liberal Party lies the
real danger to the Home Rule cause.'[43.]
Eventually tempers cooled, partly because the Liberals lost
much of their enthusiasm for Home Rule with the death of
Gladstone. By 1905, a year before Davitt died, Hardie could
write to him:

> The strength of the enemies of Ireland in this country has lain
> in the way they have been able to excite the distrust and pas-
> sion of the British workmen against their Irish fellows, and
> nothing will surely break down this distrust... than for the
> two sections to be brought into harmonious relationships by
> working together at an election. In the last resort it is to the
> common people of Great Britain that the Irish people must
> look for... an effective measure of Home Rule.[44]

These were soothing words, reminiscent of Davitt's optimism
of the 'rising democracy of England' formulated twenty years
earlier. Yet not a great deal had happened in the two decades to
support Davitt. Only the marxist influence to the left of
Labourism and the Liberal inheritance on its right had given
much hope to the Irish. At least the questions had been introduced
into the consciousness of British Labour. Why should British
socialists support Irish self-determination? If they did, what

form would that self-determination take and what limitations should be placed upon it? Was not nationalism, in any form, an anathema to socialists? Could the Irish rely on British parliamentary parties to give them what they defined as freedom? Did the Irish Parliamentary Party provide an example for British Labour to follow?

Hardie's 1905 letter to Davitt had not attempted to answer these questions. It was clear though that he had a general faith that this 'common people' would, in the end come to Ireland's rescue. If Hardie's hopes echo Davitt's earlier judgement, the doubts expressed by Parnell are mirrored by those of Frederick Engels: 'You ask me,' he wrote in 1882, 'what the English workers think about colonial policy. Well, exactly the same as they think about politics in general, the same as the bourgeoisie think.'[45]

Not many of the workers referred to by Engels had, by 1900, shown any great willingness even to recognise that Ireland was a colony. On Ireland, Engel's pessimism was shared by Parnell, and a contrast to the hopes expressed by Hardie and Davitt. The years ahead would test which was the more accurate assessment.

2. 'A Detached Party'

In 1901, the first annual conference of the Labour Representation Committee, soon to become the Labour Party, unanimously agreed:

> That, inasmuch as modern imperialism with its attendent militarism is a reversion to one of the worst phases of barbarianism; is inimical to social reform and disastrous to trade and commerce; a fruitful cause of war; destructive of freedom; fraught with menace to representative institutions at home and abroad; and must end in the destruction of democracy; this congress desires most earnestly to impress upon the working class the urgent need there is for combatting this dangerous and barbaric development in all its manifestations.[1]

'Imperialism' in this context was a pejorative, rather than a scientific description. The Labour Party had emerged just as the British Empire had experienced its most spectacular expansion. The Labour pioneers had shown little willingness to oppose in practice that expansion; they preferred to demand that its fruits be spread more evenly among the residents of the home nation. There was no recognition that Britain's hold on Ireland had an imperialist or even a colonial motivation. That may be one reason why, with the death of Gladstone, Irish Home Rule tumbled down the table of the Liberal Party's priorities.

The infant Labour Party copied the Liberals in that respect, as they did in so many others. There grew up among Labour's leaders a sense of boredom with the whole business, and an unwillingness for the party to have an official position. 'Imperialism', when it was ritually denounced, was what happened in Africa and India, not in Ireland. Thus, in 1905, when the Kettering and District Trades Council wrote to Ramsay MacDonald to say that it 'had always considered Home Rule as part of the Labour Representation Committee's programme', MacDonald asked: 'On what grounds?'[2]

MacDonald's reply to the Kettering letter stemmed not just from his position as secretary of the LRC, but also from his participation in a by-election in North Belfast in September 1905, when he served as agent for the Labour candidate William Walker. That poll provided the first public scrutiny of Labour's attitude towards Irish Home Rule.

In 1905 William Walker was one of the best known trade unionists and socialists in Ireland. He had been among the leadership of Belfast Trades Council, president of the Irish Trades Union Congress, was a member of the Independent Labour Party, a delegate to the early conferences of the LRC and had been, and was to be again, a member of the executive. He was also, however, a determined opponent of Irish Home Rule. His by-election propaganda emphasised this to the North Belfast electorate, the majority of whom were Protestant and Unionist. The first policy on his election address insisted, in bold type that: 'As a Unionist', the voters could depend on Walker's 'hostility to any measure of Home Rule'.[3] All his election material was aimed at the Protestant voters, although there were 1,000 Catholic electors in the constituency: 'Vote for Walker and show the English workmen that besides being Unionist you are also in favour of social reforms', was the plea in one leaflet.[4] Another, dealing with the Unionist candidate Sir Daniel Dixon, complained: 'It is not Patriotism, not Unionism, not... Protestantism that Sir Daniel Dixon defends.'[5]

In replies to a questionnaire from the Belfast Protestant Association (BPA), Walker pledged to 'resist every effort to throw open the offices of the Lord Chancellor of England and the Lord Lieutenant of Ireland to Roman Catholics'; to 'contend against every proposal to open diplomatic relations between the Vatican and the Court of St James'; to 'resist every attack upon the legislative enactments provided by our forefathers as necessary safeguards against the encroachment of the Papacy'.[6]

Walker's anti-Home Rule stance caused something of a stir in Labour circles in Britain. Letters of protest arrived at the LRC headquarters from a variety of organisations. These included the executive of the Amalgamated Society of Railway Servants, the Warrington Trades and Labour Council, the London branch of the Society of Coachmakers, the Coventry Trades and Labour Council, the executive of the Dock, Wharf, Riverside and General Workers' Union and the North Staffordshire Trades and Labour Council.

Other attacks were made publically. Ben Turner, president of the General Union of Textile Workers, writing in *Cotton Factory Times*, noted that 'all those on the national committee of the LRC' were 'pronounced Home Rulers, and declared: 'In the Labour Party are many who are ardent Home Rulers, and a few who are not. Democracy calls for freedom of nations to rule themselves. Ireland is a nation; therefore Mr Walker's anti-Home Rule spirit was wrong from the LRC point of view.'[7]

Similar criticisms came from the LRC executive member Pete Curran, who wrote in the *Daily News* on 18 September:

> There is a very broad principle underlying this matter. In the first place, to be politically a democrat one must recognise the necessity for decentralisation of government and, while Ireland has the first claim to self-government for two reasons — the first because the overwhelming majority of her representatives demand it; secondly because of her geographical position — the same claim can, and will be put forth in days to come by Scotland and Wales. A Labour group in parliament would no doubt go strong for devolution of government on these lines...
>
> It is essentially a Labour question, because it is evident that the industrial resources of Ireland will never be thoroughly developed until the question of self-government be settled once and for all. I would at least regard it as a duty of every Labour representative, Irish and British, to work for the settlement of the Irish political problem... from the standpoint of democratic principle.

Ramsay MacDonald attempted to defend Walker. Not by a political endorsement of Unionism, but on the basis that the LRC had no declared policy on Home Rule. He wrote to Ben Turner, complaining about the article in *Cotton Factory Times:*

> However much one might personally object to Walker's Unionism he was perfectly entitled under our constitution to explain his position to any question that he thought fit and to make his explanation in such a way as did not suit us individually, provided, of course, that the question was not one upon which Labour had made an official pronouncement.[8]

MacDonald's arguments were accepted by the LRC executive at its meeting on 4 October 1905. Walker, it was decided, had 'broken no provision of the LRC constitution', but the executive did rap Walker over the knuckles for his answers to the Belfast Protestant Association questionnaire: 'It was improper to accentuate religious strife during the contest.'[9]

It has been suggested by one contemporary colleague that MacDonald's attitude towards the Irish question was coloured by a 'dislike of papal influence'.[10] But in a personal letter to Irish socialist Tom Johnson, MacDonald maintained:

> My own feeling has been that the business was muddled from beginning to end. I was never more sick of an election than that at North Belfast, and then the religious replies coming at the back of it knocked everything out of me. I am afraid these answers will make it impossible for Mr Walker to win the constituency.[11]

Walker lost the election and subsequent contests.

Whatever the nature of MacDonald's private thoughts, he had felt obliged to make a public defence of Walker. Not only was he Walker's agent during the election, but the LRC executive had endorsed the candidate's manifesto in advance, including his description of himself as a Unionist. Whether the executive was constitutionally correct in doing so is questionable. Although the LRC had not debated Ireland at its conferences, its 1900 General Election manifesto had pledged the party to supporting 'legislative independence for all parts of the Empire'.

The Walker affair did not open a discussion within the Labour Party on what its official position on Ireland should be. Attempts to criticise Walker were ruled out of order at the 1906 party conference and the election manifesto of that year offered no commitment to Home Rule, nor indeed did it even mention Ireland.

The majority of the election addresses of the LRC-endorsed candidates did not toe this silent line. Forty of the 50 candidates made some commitment to some form of Irish Home Rule, although at least two of the abstainers were well-known candidates. Arther Henderson, the chairman of the LRC, standing in a Durham constituency and Philip Snowden, another leading personality, standing in Blackburn, made no mention of the issue. A variety of formulations were used by those who did endorse some form of Irish self-determination. Most common were phrases like 'Home Rule for Ireland', with other candidates, such as those in Halifax, Northfleet, Bolton and Wakefield, extending the principle to devolved parliaments in England, Scotland and Wales. Some candidates were more ambiguous. In Barrow-in-Furness there was support for 'gradually extending to the Irish people a great measure of participation in their domestic affairs'. The candidate in Woolwich, while supporting 'the largest possible share of self-government' for Ireland, added: 'England would be the gainer by the withdrawal of an unwise and irksome influence'.

Other phraseology employed included the Southampton candidate's support for Irish 'national autonomy', the Darlington candidate's, 'entrusting the Irish people with the management of their own affairs' and Keir Hardie's pledge in Merthyr Tydfil that he would 'support the demand of the Irish Party'.

The 1906 election marked a substantial advance for the Labour Party, as the LRC now became. It won 29 seats. Among those elected were Hardie, MacDonald, Snowden, Henderson and J.R. Clynes, all of whom were to have some influence in establishing an Irish policy for the party. MacDonald replaced Hardie as leader, being judged more dependable and less militant by the trade union officials. But Hardie summed up the mood of the parliamentary party as well as anyone when he wrote in 1910 that party members needed to prove themselves, 'statesmen as well as agitators'.[12]

The election was won by the Liberals who obtained a Commons majority of 84. The Irish Nationalists were among the other parties represented, but the size of the government majority meant that it was not at the mercy of Irish Nationalist votes. Accordingly, the Irish question was omitted from parliamentary deliberations, although it occasionally intruded into Labour's affairs. When Walker again stood unsuccessfully in North Belfast in a 1907 by-election, Labour's executive reported to that year's conference:

> At the time of the contest there was much political unsettlement in the North of Ireland caused by rumours that the government intended introducing a Home Rule Bill, and this seriously influenced the polling of a straight Labour vote and drew out maximum support for the Unionist candidate.[13]

This was an important, if obvious evaluation. If it needed only a rumour to push the Protestant workers into the Conservative and Unionist camp, then how sustainable was the cause of Labour among those workers, especially when the party maintained an ambiguity on Home Rule and declined to debate the subject year after year?

At the 1907 Labour Party conference, held in Belfast, C. Greig of the city's trades council, warned against such discussions:

> If any of the delegates during their stay here wished to study Belfast politics, they would find the study an interesting one. If, however, they wanted to master them more thoroughly their stay in Belfast would have to be longer than the weekend.[14]

The conference report noted that these words were greeted with laughter, and then the delegates moved on to discuss more pressing matters, such as cab trade legislation, postman's hours, vaccination, shop registration, payment of juries and the laws governing motor traffic. All these issues were debated at the first ten conferences of the LRC/Labour Party. Ireland was not.

Labour's early disinterest in the national aspirations of the Irish majority was reciprocated. By 1910 the only Irish affiliate to the party was the Belfast trades council, although as early as 1903 the Irish Trades Union Congress (ITUC) had passed a resolution recommending that the trade unions in Ireland affiliate to the LRC.

That decision was reaffirmed a number of times in the following ten years, but it was not one which went uncontested. Two other options for the ITUC were canvassed. One, which had been accepted a year before the 1903 vote, called for 'a pledge bound labour party, controlled by and answerable to the Irish TUC'.[15] This debate, whether Irish labour should form their own party or be part of British Labour's political organisation, was one repeatedly, and sometimes bitterly debated in Ireland from 1900 to 1912. The most famous example was a public polemic between Connolly and Walker, which in essence centred around the attitude socialists in Ireland should have towards the link with Britain.[16]

The other political possibility considered by Irish trade unionists in the early years of the twentieth century was to look to the Irish Nationalists at Westminster to advance the cause of Irish labour.

The dispute was not settled until 1912 when a definitive position in favour of an 'independent Labour Party in Ireland' was adopted.[17] The decision caused a good deal of friction between the representatives of Irish and British labour, as will be seen shortly, but by and large the British Labour Party took no part in, and paid little interest to the theoretical debates around socialism and the Irish national question. Even the Independent Labour Party, supposedly the more socialist section of the Labour Party, devoted no conference time during these years to a thorough debate on Ireland, and produced no pamphlet or policy statement on the subject.

On the rare occasions when the issue was raised, the Labour leaders reacted with exasperation. When the Irish trade union leader and syndicalist, James Larkin, attended the 1908 ILP conference and 'voiced the grievances of Ireland', Ramsay MacDonald advised the delegates that although Larkin had been 'a little provocative... we must take no notice of it'.[18]

There was a price to be paid for such neglect. Electoral advancement, a yardstick valued above all others by the Labour Party, suffered. Keir Hardie complained in his presidential address to the Labour Party conference of 1910: 'The executive of the Irish National League of Great Britain saw fit to order the Irish vote in nearly every three-cornered contest to be cast on the side of the Liberal candidate'.[19]

For Hardie, 'the reason' for this decision was 'not apparent', but to anyone not blinded by the parochial concerns of British labourism the reasons were obvious. Hardie himself provided one when, in his same presidential address, he insisted:

> In the last resort the claims of the Irish people can only be won by the working class of Great Britain rallying to their support, and it does not appear to me that this is likely to be hastened by the leaders of an Irish organisation this side of the channel using their power to bludgeon down Labour candidates.

If the suggestion that Irish self-determination would only come when the British Labour was ready to throw its weight behind the cause was true, then there was little hope for the Irish. The party's manifestos in the two general elections of 1910 again made no commitment to, nor mention of Irish Home Rule. There was also a decreasing adherence to Home Rule in the 1910 election addresses of Labour candidates. Of the 51 which survive in the Labour Party library, 33 expressed support, 17 made no reference to the topic and one was ambiguous.

This swing away from Home Rule by Labour candidates proved short-sighted when the results of the two 1910 elections again made legislation on Home Rule a real possibility. After the December count, the Liberals and Conservatives had the same number of seats in parliament, with 42 Labour and 84 Irish Nationalists holding the balance of power. To rule the British, the Liberals had to satisfy the Irish. The chief consequence of the election was to limit the power of the House of Lords, which effectively had killed Gladstone's attempts to pass Home Rule. The Irish question seemed, at last, to demand a positive answer.

Officially, the Labour Party's position on Home Rule was no different than it had been in 1905 when MacDonald underlined the abstentionist position during the William Walker controversy. Yet, when the Liberals did eventually present their Government of Ireland Bill to parliament early in 1912, James Parker rose in the Commons to endorse the measure on behalf of Labour. There was no hint of past equivocation in his words:

> I have known most of the members of the Labour Party for ten to twenty years, and I believe there is not a man amongst them who has not been an advocate of Home Rule for years before he came to this House. So far as I know they would risk their seats tomorrow for Home Rule for Ireland, and believe that in so doing they were fighting for a principle of political reform and a forerunner of social reform as far as Ireland is concerned. What is the first essential of government? Applied to a nation it is that it shall be governed in the manner in which it desires: government of the people, for the people, by the people...
>
> So far as the Labour Party is concerned, we stand for Home Rule because we believe that the mass of working people of Ireland have a right to decide what form of government they shall have, and because when they have that form of government they will themselves carry out their own social reform in a manner which suits them best.[20]

Parker was not a particularly prominent member of the Parliamentary Labour Party, and in that respect it is noteworthy that it was he and not MacDonald, Snowden, J.H. Thomas or any of the better known Labour leaders who spoke in the first stages of the debate.

Parker's reference to the personal support for Irish Rule offered by the Labour MPs was probably accurate. The Liberal
inheritance which many of these MPs shared and the small influence of the marxists both pushed in that direction. But this
does not disguise the fact that Parker was speaking on behalf of
the Parliamentary Labour Party and not for the party as a
whole.

In addition, among the leaders of the party the feeling remained that the whole issue should be dispensed with as soon as
possible to allow consideration of the more bread and butter
issues dominating the consciousness of Labour workers. The
parliamentary report presented to the 1913 Labour conference
reflected this attitude:

> The session has been mainly taken up with fulfilling pledges
> given in respect of three big political measures, two of which
> were the Home Rule and Welsh Disestablishment Bills. In
> respect to these the Party generally had made most definite
> promises to the constituencies and it did its best to get the
> measures carried and put out of the way.[21]

The wording of this report was obviously chosen with care.
The phrase 'promises to the constituencies' was the justification
offered for Labour adopting its new parliamentary position on
Home Rule. Even that argument is suspect when it is recalled
that more than one third of Labour election addresses in
December 1910 had not endorsed Home Rule. This many have
been one reason why the parliamentary leaders felt they had to
further justify their support of it to the 1913 conference. The
presidential address given by George Roberts MP explained:

> Consistent support has been given to the national aspirations
> of the Irish and Welsh democracies. This was motivated both
> by an appreciation of their merits and an anxiety to clear the
> political stage, and thereby enhance the prospect of the pur-
> poses which more immediately concern us.[22]

Both reports were accepted by conference and the Labour Party
at last had an official policy on the Irish question.

Unfortunately for Labour the question being asked was
rapidly changing. An indication of the difficulty came at a
meeting between representatives of the Irish TUC and the

Labour Party leaders Ramsay MacDonald and Arthur Henderson in July 1913. Relations between the organisations of Irish and British labour had been worsening for some time. The 1913 conference of the Irish TUC had reaffirmed its decision of the previous year to form its own political party, but the parliamentary committee of the Irish TUC had also reported in 1913 the wish of the British Labour Party that the new Irish organisation should be no more than a branch of its British counterpart.

Consequently the meeting in July 1913 was an intemperate affair. The Irish went on the offensive, vigorously defending their right to form a separate party and accusing the British Labour Party of 'taking counsel with the Irish Nationalist Party on labour matters or on questions affecting the workers in Ireland, over the heads of the representatives of the Irish Trades Congress'.[23]

The complaint was justifiable. The Parliamentary Labour Party, whose founders had politically grown up with the model of the Irish Parliamentary Party constantly before them, continued to regard its successor with high respect. Whenever the Irish TUC forwarded resolutions to the Labour Party its leaders in parliament referred them to the Irish Nationalists in the Commons for endorsement or rejection.

MacDonald and Henderson defended this procedure when they met the Irish TUC, saying they regarded the Irish Nationalists as the genuine representatives of the Irish people. They refused to guarantee that in future they would consult the 'Irish labour movement' on Irish affairs.

This would have been a strong argument if the Irish MPs had indeed been the political arbiters of Irish self-determination. But as any close observer of Irish politics from 1912 onwards could perceive this was already becoming doubtful. Anyway, whatever the relative support for Irish labour or Irish Nationalists at home, the political instinct of the British Labour Party was to lean towards an endorsement of the Nationalists' Home Rule rather than Irish labour's advocation of separation. Similarly, for the leaders of the Labour Party it went against the grain to approve a separate Irish Labour Party. When the Irish TUC asked that a portion of the political levy collected by British trade unions organising in Ireland be paid into the new Irish party instead of going in its entirety to the British Labour

Party, MacDonald and Henderson refused. Referring to this meeting four years later, Henderson, in a letter to the Irish TUC, showed an unrepentive sarcasm: 'And we have been aware of your desire to run your own Labour Party independent of everything British, as was very frankly stated when I was in conference with your representatives four years ago'.[24]

The differences between the political representatives of British labour and their Irish counterparts, headed by Larkin and Connolly, were not confined to the degree of Irish self-determination which was desirable. The whole direction the Irish movement was taking was in militant contrast to the sober deference to constitutionalism displayed by most of the leaders of the Labour Party and TUC. At no time was the dichotomy more apparent than during the great Dublin lock-out which began in September 1913.

The detailed history of that dispute cannot be retold here.[25] Suffice to say that on one level it was an industrial dispute about the right to organise but it was at the same time the most militant conflict ever seen in Ireland or Britain. One which opened up the prospect of a workers' revolution. That outcome was ruled out, not least because of the attitude of the leaders of the British Labour Party and the TUC, who refused the appeals of Larkin and Connolly for both the blacking of all goods from England to the Irish employers and for widespread sympathetic strike action on the mainland.

The deaf ears in Britain were assailed with many choice words from across the water. Larkin called MacDonald and Philip Snowden 'serpents',[26] and J.H, Thomas a 'class traitor'.[27] Connolly called the British union leaders 'old fossils... willing to sell the pass any time'.[28]

The replies of MacDonald, Snowden and others were couched in more diplomatic language. MacDonald said a sympathy strike would be 'poor fighting'[29] and said the syndicalism of James Larkin was '15 years out of date'.[30] Snowden's view was that the Dublin trade unions were 'undisciplined and dangerous'.[31]

At the heart of the dispute was a profound disagreement over the meaning of socialism and how it could be attained. On one side were Connolly, a revolutionary socialist, and Larkin, a syndicalist. Facing them were MacDonald, Snowden and Henderson who preached constitutionalism, parliamentarianism and the capacity of the British capitalist system to reform itself if enough polite lobbying was mounted.

The differences were not just theoretical. Larkin and Connolly threatened to set an example capable of being followed by the rank and file of British labour on whom MacDonald and his fellow leaders depended for support. Trade union and Labour Party branches complained to MacDonald that the Labour Party was not doing enough to help the Irish,[32] and when Larkin and Connolly spoke in Britain they often drew vast crowds. Larkin attracted nearly 25,000 to one Manchester meeting.[33]

The leaders of the Labour Party and TUC survived the challenge of Larkin and Connolly, but that was by no means the end of the Parliamentary Labour Party's Irish troubles. The militancy of Larkin and Connolly was only one manifestation of an Ireland which seemed to be becoming more and more ungovernable, due to the tensions that had risen in Ireland and Britain as a consequence of the Liberals' Government of Ireland Bill.

The Bill was an exercise in caution. Ireland was to be given a separate parliament but with strictly limited powers. Westminster, at which Irish MPs would continue to sit, would retain control over defence, foreign relations, custom and excise and all major aspects of financial revenue. The imperial parliament would retain complete authority over the Irish police for six years.

Yet, for John Redmond, the leader of the Irish Nationalists in Parliament, the Bill was 'a great measure... a great measure'.[34] For Edward Carson, who by then had become leader of the Irish Unionists, it was, 'the most nefarious conspiracy that has ever been hatched against a free people'.[35] For Bonar Law, leader of the British Conservative opposition: 'I can imagine no length of resistance of which Ulster can go in which I should not be prepared to support them.'[36]

The north of Ireland resistance Bonar Law had in mind was evident early in 1913 with the founding of the Ulster Volunteer Force (UVF), the 'armed wing' of Unionists in Ulster. By March, 1914 it had a membership of 85,000 and, according to a police estimate, 21,000 guns. It paraded and drilled openly, led by former British Army officers and encouraged by prominent Unionist and Conservative politicians. It was a physical reminder of the sentiments expressed in the Ulster Covenant, a declaration launched in September 1912 in which nearly 450,000 people had pledged to 'use all means which may be found necessary to defeat the present conspiracy to set up a Home Rule Parliament in Ireland'.

On the heels of the UVF came the Irish Volunteers formed in the south of the country. Their objective was to 'secure and maintain the rights and liberties common to all the people of Ireland'. Though less openly aggressive and not as well armed as the UVF, the Irish Volunteers were also a reflection of the trend in Ireland towards direct action. A further manifestation was the tiny Citizen Army, formed by Connolly and Larkin during the Dublin lock-out.

Considering the limited nature of the Government of Ireland Bill, this rush to arms, or at least training, could be viewed as an over-reaction. But as John Redmond said, the Bill was 'a provisional settlement' which allowed 'time for revision'.[37] Accordingly, all sides saw that there was more at stake than the mild palliative for Ireland's ills that was contained in the actual legislation. For the Nationalists, the Bill was a door which could open up greater freedoms; for the Unionists those freedoms would be won at the expense of the political, economic and social privileges they had enjoyed for so long in Ireland; for the Tories and British Army officers the indivisibility of the British Empire was at stake.

In contrast, the British Labour Party refused to get excited. When the second reading of the Bill went through parliament in June 1913, James O'Grady, on behalf of the Labour Party, almost apologised for intervening in the debate, explaining that the party 'cannot allow this occason to pass' without 'offering a few remarks on behalf of the party with which I am associated'.[38] Indeed O'Grady felt it was necessary to 'remind the House that the British majority in this House in favour of Home Rule includes the 40 Labour members'.

O'Grady, who had spent 15 years as a union organiser in Belfast, devoted most of his speech to the Ulster question:

> How have these honourable members from Ulster got together these great bodies of workmen to protest against Home Rule? They are not protesting against Home Rule. They are not protesting Home Rule at all. They are inveigled together to join a combination on the assumption that the

Protestant faith is going to be persecuted with all the vigour
that a government might foolishly enact, and I complain
against honourable members when it is a known fact that during the last ten years in particular the growth of the labour
movement in the town of Belfast has done more to bring
Catholic and Protestant workmen together to vote upon pure
economic issues in political concerns than any other movement that has taken place, that they should come together to
seek to rend the movement by dividing these men into Protestant and Catholic.[39]

This description of the Belfast labour movement over the
previous decade was an exaggeration. Since 1907 it had been in
decline in the areas of both political and industrial organisation.
By July 1913, Connolly, then a union organiser in Belfast, was
complaining that 'the feeling of the city is so violently Orange'
that his task, as a representative of an Irish based trade union,
'has been a hard one all along'.[40]

Also unlikely is the implication in O'Grady's remarks that
the Unionist ruling class had used the Government of Ireland
Bill to conspire to divide the Belfast working class. The truth
was that this working class had been divided years before the
Liberals had announced their intention of passing Home Rule.
Those divisions, while certainly encouraged and inflamed by the
rich and powerful in the Unionist leadership, were very concrete.
They were based on the marginal economic privileges the Protestant working class enjoyed over their Catholic counterparts in
Belfast and elsewhere in Ireland and they were reinforced by a
whole series of ideological influences.[41]

The Labour Party had always shied away from discussing
and analysing these working class divisions. Accordingly, it had
made no attempt to counter them, preferring to dismiss them in
the manner of the simplistic notions evident in O'Grady's
remarks. The party representatives argued, when they bothered
to apply their minds to the subject, that Home Rule was no more
than a necessary reform, unexceptional in its implications, good
for the Irish working class, good for Ireland and good for Britain.
For O'Grady, the Irish

are the only white race under the British flag that has been
denied the right of self-government. Have the honourable
members opposed to this Bill ever considered why the British
Empire is so strong and so unified as it is? ...I believe that it is

because the British Empire, as no empire that ever existed before ever was, is based upon a foundation of self-governing states, and that it could not exist without that basis.[42]

O'Grady was the only Labour speaker during the second reading of the Bill, successfully carried in the Commons but rejected by the House of Lords. Under the terms of the recently passed Parliament Act, which had restricted the powers of the Lords, the Bill was still due to become law in 1914.

The extra-parliamentary conspiracy to defeat the Bill got underway in earnest. Edward Carson and his Unionists were openly threatening rebellion. They were supported by the Conservatives, whose leader Bonar Law declared: 'There are things stronger than parliamentary majorities'.[43] Most importantly, many of the leading officers in the British Army allied themselves with the Unionists. The most dramatic evidence of that allegiance came in March 1914 when 58 officers at the Currage barracks near Dublin proffered their resignations rather than face the prospect of being ordered to move against an Ulster rebellion. A month later the apparent helplessness of the government was displayed when 20,000 rifles and 3,000,000 rounds of ammunition were delivered to the UVF via ports in the north-east of Ireland.

Inevitably, the Liberal government, unsure how effective any military move against the Ulster Unionists would be and politically unwilling to attempt any such move, began to consider a compromise on the Government of Ireland Bill. An amendment which would allow any county in Ulster to opt out of the jurisdiction of an Irish parliament for up to six years was introduced. Referring to this proposal in the Commons in March 1914, Ramsay MacDonald declared:

So far as the Labour Party is concerned, we are quite immovable. The first question is: Is Ulster to deny the rights of the rest of Ireland to self-government? We say, 'No, emphatically not'. Arising out of that, and a somewhat narrower question is this: 'Is Ulster going to deny the right of Ireland ever to speak and to act as a unified nationality? We say, 'No, emphatically not'. The third point is: Has this House now the right to settle the question? We say emphatically that it has, and I hope that there is going to be no mistake about it...

I am sure that, so far as every section of this House is concerned, we would desire it to go through under conditions of peace. We should desire that there should be agreement within the limits and confines of Home Rule; and so far as we are concerned here we do not propose to interfere. It is not our business. If there is going to be a six year limit acceptable to the honourable members opposite, both sections, very well, we may have our opinions about their wisdom or lack of wisdom, but our votes and our voices will not prevent their coming to an agreement...

We will take the position of a detached party listening to what is said, and noticing what is said, helping, as we have done during the last two years in every possible way, Home Rule to be inscribed on the statute book of this realm.[44]

The meaning of this speech needs to be clarified, for there was much sleight of hand at work in the words chosen. At first glance it appears that MacDonald's attitude to partition was 'emphatically not'. But this was qualified by the use of the word 'ever' in opposing the 'right' of Ulster to veto a united Ireland. In other words, not for ever, but for six years, possibly. And if such a concession was acceptable to the Unionists and Nationalists then Labour would 'not interfere'. It was, at best, an abstentionist position, the view of a 'detached party', which, nevertheless, stressed that any Irish settlement must remain within 'the limits and confines of Home Rule'. This detachment was reaffirmed by another Labour speaker, J.E. Sutton, who suggested that while 'we on these benches believe in majority rule', and that 'the majority in Ireland are in favour of this Bill', the whole business was something of a nuisance because 'so long as Home Rule is being discussed year after year, questions of social reform, affecting the interests of workers, are constantly being neglected'.[45]

There is no evidence to suggest that the Labour Party at large sought to distance itself from the apathy towards Ireland shown by its parliamentary representatives. During these years the occasional resolution was forwarded to the party conference but there was no debate and no great demand for one from the party rank and file.

Labour's executive committee minutes during the period show that the only time there was even a hint of rebellion from local parties on the Irish issue was over the leadership's lack of solidarity during the 1913 Dublin lock-out — and that was seen as a trade union issue having no relevance to the national question.

The reasons for this lack of interest both in and out of parliament are not hard to establish: an acceptance that the role of Labour was to win social and economic reforms, and that it had no other mandate; a belief that Home Rule was inevitable and therefore not worth expending great energy; and a growing divergence between the British and Irish labour movements whereby the British Labour Party had hidden from itself the real situation in Ireland and where that was leading.

Perhaps there was another factor at work, discernible in MacDonald's remarks about making 'no mistake' that parliament should, once and for all, decide the matter. What occurred in those two years before the first world war challenged a belief fundamental to the Labour Party; i.e. that everything could be achieved by the securing of a simple parliamentary majority. The Ulster rebellion demonstrated otherwise.

By the time the war broke out, the government had failed to deliver Home Rule, despite the wishes of the majority of the Irish and despite majority support in the House of Commons. Moreover, by proposing the right of Ulster counties to opt out of a united Ireland, albeit for only six years, the principle of partition had been accepted, although not one vote in Britain or Ireland had ever endorsed such a solution. There was of course no guarantee that six years would not stretch to sixteen or sixty years.

All this had happened because of the threat of armed rebellion by the Unionists, supported by the highest levels of the Conservative Party and assisted by the elite of the British Army. Against such an alliance the House of Commons became almost a spectator. It was certainly unwilling to take up this challenge to its authority. If the British Labour Party leaders had thought about it — just where did it leave their veneration of parliamentarism?

Many in Ireland did draw the obvious conclusion. When, at the outbreak of the war, John Redmond committed the Irish Volunteers to the British Army, the Volunteers split. Although the majority followed Redmond, his prestige, and that of his party was now on the wane. Indeed it had been for some time. The decision of the Irish TUC to establish its own political party in 1912 was one of the many examples of the growing appeal of a separatist ideology in Ireland. The failure of the Government of Ireland Bill intensified that appeal.

For some, like James Connolly, the prospect of partition

was so catastrophic that desperate measures were not necessary. Connolly's socialism told him what would be the consequences of dividing Ireland:

> Such a scheme... the betrayal of the national democracy of Industrial Ulster, would mean a carnival of reaction both North and South, would set back the wheels of progress, would destroy the oncoming unity of the Irish labour movement and paralyse all advanced movements while it lasted.[46]

That statement explains one of the impulses that led Connolly to participate in the Easter Rising of 1916 when the Irish Republic was proclaimed from the steps of the General Post Office in Dublin. What concerns us here about the Rising and its consequences is that it marked the nadir of the relationship between socialists in Ireland and their parliamentary counterparts in Britain. Labour MPs sat in the wartime coalition Cabinet which executed Connolly and his comrades. Indeed Labour Cabinet member, Arthur Henderson, was reported to have cheered when the executions of Padraic Pearse, Tom Clarke and Thomas MacDonagh were announced in the House of Commons.[47] Just before his execution Connolly had predicted that socialists 'will never understand why I am here'.[48] Initially that was certainly the case for many Irish socialists, most European ones and the vast majority in Britain.

J.H. Thomas, the British Labour Party's old adversary of Connolly and Larkin, wrote in a newspaper article in May 1916: 'There was no Labour leader in this country who did not deplore the recent rebellion in Ireland. They look upon it with sorrow and amazement'.[49]

The British labour movement's own newspaper, the *Daily Herald* editorialised: 'No lover of peace can do anything but deplore the outbreak in Dublin'.[50] The journal of the Independent Labour Party shielded behind its pacifism in September 1916: 'In no degree do we approve the Sinn Fein rebellion. We do not approve of armed rebellion at all, any more than other forms of militarism'.[51] And the parliamentary report given to the Labour Party conference of 1917 confined itself to describing the Rising as 'the calamitous outbreak'.[52] On the Easter Rising, the voice of the Labour Party spoke of Ireland with a rare strength, unanimity and without equivocation.

3. The Search for a Policy

The 1916 Easter Rising led George Bernard Shaw to write to the Liberal *Daily News*:

> My own view is that the men who were shot in cold blood...
> were prisoners of war, and that it was therefore entirely incor-
> rect to shoot them...
>   Until Dublin Castle is superceded by a national parliament
> and Ireland voluntarily incorporated with the British Empire,
> as Canada, Australasia and South Africa have been incor-
> porated, an Irishman resorting to arms to achieve in-
> dependence of his country is only doing what Englishmen will
> do, if it be their misfortune to be invaded and conquered.[1]

This was Shaw the Irishman, rather than Shaw the Fabian, speaking. Few socialists in England, and certainly not those of the Fabian variety, contemplated breaking the consensus of condemnation which greeted the Rising.

Those who did tended to have been born in Ireland. In October 1916 James O'Grady made what was for a Labour MP so exceptional a speech, that it deserves quoting at some length:

> Let me go back to some of the people in the rebellion. I knew
> some of the men who were, unfortunately, executed by the
> British government. I knew them to be absolutely sincere.
> They always declared themselves to be what they were — the
> enemies of English rule in Ireland, and they died enemies of
> that rule in Ireland. I always thought that it was one of the
> characteristics of the British race to have some regard for a
> man who has the courage of his convictions, and that in cir-
> cumstances like these they would have taken the human
> view... would not have gone to the extent of executing these
> men. I have been told, and I give it for what it was worth, that
> when a friend of mine [James Connolly] was brought before a
> court martial and condemned to death, his condition was such
> that the officers themselves appealed for him that he should
> put in a plea for mercy... He told the officers that he was

going to die as he had lived, always the enemy of British rule in Ireland. Whatever mistaken views a man may have... I do suggest that to treat a man like that, under circumstances such as existed in Ireland at the time of his death, is an unwise act of statesmanship, apart from the mere question of the human aspect...

Englishmen never can and never will understand Ireland. It is a question of psychology, as well as a question of politics and justice. You have never attempted to understand Ireland. At least, Englishmen have never attempted to understand Irishmen from that point of view.[2]

O'Grady was speaking during a debate on a censure motion, proposed by the Nationalists, condemning the government's operation of martial law in Ireland. He said he was 'speaking on behalf of my colleagues on these benches', but although the bulk of his speech criticised the government for playing into the hands of Sinn Fein by its repressive policies, even this qualified criticism was not endorsed by the Parliamentary Labour Party. When the vote on the censure motion was taken, less than half of the Labour MPs participated; 15 voted for and three voted against.

Less than a year after the abortive uprising, the Home Rule movement and its parliamentary representatives were on their way to becoming a part of history. The new times were heralded at the Ruscommon by-election in the west of Ireland on 4 February 1917, when the Sinn Fein candidate, Count Plunkett, father of an executed leader of the Rising, defeated the Nationalist candidate by 3,022 votes to 1,702. The advocates of Home Rule suffered a similar defeat at the hands of proponents of full independence in South Longford in April. In the same month a meeting of the British Cabinet acknowledged: 'The Home Rule Act is, in certain respects, out of date and, in any circumstances and by common consent, must be amended before it can come into operation'.[3]

The Parliamentary Labour Party offered condolences. The 1917 party conference was told that the PLP 'deplores the failure to give legislative effect to the temporary settlement of the Home Rule controversy', and that it 'desires to express its entire sympathy with the Nationalist Party in the repeated postponement of plans to realise their own national aims'.[4]

What those 'national aims' constituted and the attitude the

Labour Party should have towards them were to be the subject of internal controversy over the next four years. In the meantime, however much 'sympathy' the PLP expressed towards the Nationalists, Labour was backing a crippled horse. Perhaps if the forty or so Labour MPs had applied greater pressure on the government to stand up to the Unionist rebellion in the years 1912-14 they would not have been faced in 1917 with a Nationalist Party — which they had admired for so long — that had become irrelevant.

The war in Europe intensified Labour's helplessness. Despite O'Grady's harsh criticism in October 1916 he had assured the government that 'though I am speaking like this, and speaking in the name of my own party on the general question, we shall not do anything to prevent or to embarrass this government in carrying on the war'.[5] A year later O'Grady himself was to experience the impossibility of separating the Irish question from the conduct of the war.

By then the war was going particularly badly for Britain. Things were made worse by the Russian revolution and the departure of Russia from the war in November 1917. Shortly before the new Communist government took that decision, O'Grady had visited the Soviet Union. He reported his purpose and his impressions to the House of Commons on 23 October 1917 in an intriguing and neglected reference:

> When I was in Russia putting the case for the allies the best possible way I could, I frequently declared that Great Britain in entering the war had nothing to gain, that she did not want territory in Europe or any aggrandisement at all. I pointed out that at the beginning of the war 4,000,000 British citizens volunteered because they thought we were fighting a war of liberation. But, said some of the Russians of the soviets at Petrograd and Moscow, 'You say you are fighting a war of liberation, but what about Ireland?' The question was insistently put to us in Petrograd and Moscow and everywhere we went.[6]

O'Grady's answer was to insist that: 'The people of Great Britain are not averse to justice being rendered to Ireland', and to say that 'the real trouble was that the government of the day paid too much weight to the objections of a moiety of the Irish people'. But the attitude of the Labour Party would hardly have given much reassurance to members of the soviets. In December

1917 the national executive of the party and the parliamentary committee of the TUC drew up a 'Memorandum on War Aims'. These included, 'international trusteeship of African colonies', but no mention of Ireland.[7]

A further aspect of the Irish question had a direct bearing on Britain's war plans. This was whether conscription should be applied to the Irish.

Conscription had been in force in Britain since the beginning of 1916. A special Labour conference at the time decided to oppose it on principle but to acquiesce in practice, avoiding embarrassing those Labour MPs who had served in the coalition Cabinet since May 1915, the most prominent of whom was Arthur Henderson. Although Henderson was forced out of the government in August 1917, Labour continued to be represented in the Cabinet up until November 1918.

Accordingly, the party had a direct interest in the Military Service Bill, introduced in April 1918. Its most dramatic clause was a proposal to extend conscription to Ireland, where large parts of the country were already in a state of semi-insurrection. A government report noted that by March 1918 Sinn Fein had more than 80,000 members and that 'mere boys now defy the police, and when charged in court declare themselves citizens of the Irish Republic or soldiers of the Irish Republican Army and refuse to acknowledge the jurisdiction of the magistrates'.[8] Even General Sir Brian Mahon, commanding officer of the British Army in Ireland, reported that

> conscription can be enforced but with the greatest difficulty... The present time is the worst for it since I have been in Ireland... I would suggest that the first thing is to get all known leaders out of the way at once, extra troops should be on the spot immediately, and everyone, irrespective of who he is, arrested on the first sign of giving trouble.[9]

Such reports led to a long and hard debate in the Cabinet on whether conscription should be introduced in Ireland. Labour MP George Barnes voiced the strongest opposition, then reported to two meetings held in London on 10 April 1918. The first was between the parliamentary committee of the TUC and Labour MPs, the other when the national committee of the TUC met Labour's executive. Both meetings agreed to oppose conscription in Ireland for reasons spelled out in a memorandum submitted to the War Cabinet:

> The attempt to enforce conscription will mean not merely the shedding of the blood of thousands of Irishmen, and Englishmen and Scotmen, too; but also the maintenance of a huge, permanent army of occupation in Ireland. Today every soldier is needed at the western front; yet the government is proposing to take a course of action which will involve the withdrawal of many thousands of soldiers to engage in a civil war which will outrage the conscience of the civilised world.[10]

The memorandum claimed its appeal was 'on the grounds of principle and expediency alike', but the emphasis was on expediency, with a forecast that Britain could lose the war if an attempt was made to enforce Irish conscription. Also included was a compromise suggestion that if such a policy was adopted, then an all-Irish parliament with the right to veto conscription should be immediately convened.

This last point indicated a radical departure from earlier Labour Party policy. Support had been given to previous Home Rule Bills which specifically excluded the possibility of an Irish Home Rule parliament having the right to take decisions affecting the military security of both Ireland and Britain. The proposal for an Irish conscription veto suggested otherwise.

However, neither the party as a whole, nor its leaders, were yet ready to formally endorse such Irish self-determination. Indeed the memorandum expressed a general sentiment, rather than a declaration of policy, as became evident when Labour's executive agreed that the parliamentary party should not be bound to oppose Irish conscription in the Commons. Subsequently, when the Military Service Bill came before parliament, no Labour MP moved any amendment which would have reflected either the party's opposition to Irish conscription or to five other clauses which Labour's national committee had opposed.

Irish conscription was agreed by parliament, but it was never enforced.

The Irish controversy was now reaching crisis point. In June 1918, for the first time in its history, Labour's annual conference debated Ireland. The resolution, which was supported by the party leadership stated:

> That the conference unhesitantly recognises the claim of the people of Ireland to Home Rule and to self-determination in

all exclusively Irish affairs; it protests against the stubborn resistance to a democratic reorganisation of Irish government maintained by those who, alike in Ireland and Great Britain, are striving to keep minorities dominant; and it demands that a wide and generous measure of Home Rule... should be immediately passed into law and put into operation.[11]

The motion was moved by James O'Grady who complained that the government 'had given in to minorities', meaning the Unionists. He also came up with a revised analysis of the 1916 Easter Rising, saying that 'workers' had been 'compelled to rise in rebellion'.

Defending Easter 1916 was one thing, but what of the aim of the rebellion, the securing of a completely independent Irish Republic? The test came when N.S. Beaton, a delegate from the National Union of Shop Assistants, Warehousemen and Clerks moved an amendment to the motion which removed the proviso 'in all exclusively Irish affairs'.

This was no technical amendment, but an argument for unfettered self-determination. As such it was endorsed at the conference by Sylvia Pankhurst, a delegate from the British Socialist Party, the successor of the Social Democratic Federation which had recently reaffiliated to the Labour Party. Pankhurst pointed out: 'If they passed the resolution in preference to the amendment, they would cause the most extreme angry feeling between the Labour Party of Ireland and the Labour Party of Great Britain'.

It was true that the Irish Labour Party did have a policy of complete independence. Pankhurst's other contention that, if the amendment was lost, the conference 'would be going absolutely against the wishes of the majority of the Irish people', while not verifiable at the time, was shown to be correct six months later.

Neither consideration prevented the amendment's defeat. One delegate who voted against it warned that if Irish independence was permitted Great Britain could be threatened by an Irish army or navy. Although hardly a realistic objection given the contrast in population and resources of the two countries, this concern reflected an opinion which had been voiced before and was to continually reappear in the ranks of the party: that Irish freedom came second to British security.

By at last debating Ireland at its annual conference, Labour now at least had a formal policy which had been discussed and debated by the party as a whole, albeit briefly — only five delegates spoke in the conference debate.

Clarification was required. What exactly was meant by 'exclusively Irish affairs', and how 'wide' and how 'generous' should any Home Rule legislation be?

William Adamson, who held the chairmanship of the PLP from 1917 to 1921, offered one interpretation in July 1918 when, during a Commons debate he called for 'a measure of Home Rule as will be satisfactory to the aspirations of the Irish people'.[12] A different phraseology appeared in the Labour manifesto for the December 1918 general election where Ireland surfaced for the first time since the LRC manifesto of 1900. 'Freedom for Ireland' was the third point in the 1918 manifesto:

> The principles which Labour acclaims as Allied war aims it will apply to our own subject peoples. Freedom for Ireland and India it claims, and it will extend to all subject peoples the right of self-determination within the British Commonwealth of Nations.[13]

But what if the Irish had no wish to be part of the Commonwealth? And what if 'the aspirations of the Irish people' went beyond anything contemplated by either the House of Commons or the Labour Party? These became more than rhetorical questions when the results of the 1918 election in Ireland were declared. The Nationalists won only six out of 105 seats. The Unionists took 26, but 73 seats went to Sinn Fein — a landslide.

True to their election promises the Sinn Fein MPs, or rather the 34 who were not in British jails, absented themselves from Westminster. Instead, in January 1919, they convened Dail Eireann (Assembly of Ireland) in Dublin. A declaration of Irish independence was adopted whereby:

> We, the elected representatives of the ancient Irish people in national parliament assembled, do, in the name of the Irish nation, ratify the establishment of the Irish Republic and pledge ourselves and our people to make this declaration effective by every means at our command.

Lloyd George's coalition government reacted cautiously to this challenge. The King's speech, which opened the new British parliamentary session, said merely: 'The position in Ireland causes me great anxiety, but I earnestly hope that conditions may soon sufficiently improve to make it possible to provide a durable settlement of this difficult problem'.[14]

This example of traditional British phlegm caused some annoyance to J.R. Clynes, the new leader of the Labour Party in parliament. He comforted the House that on Ireland: 'I do not intend to say much', but went on to criticise the King's Irish reference as 'most unsatisfying... a mere pious opinion'. However, in spelling out Labour's policy towards 'this interminable Irish conflict', Clynes too failed to address his remarks to the changed Irish situation. He urged:

> In the face of divided opinion in Ireland, and the improbability of that opinion being reconciled, it becomes all the more the duty of the government to face with unusual courage the situation which has so long continued and to apply the provisions of such an Act of Parliament as this House has repeated sanctioned.[15]

As with the 1918 conference resolution and the 1918 manifesto, this was all too unspecific. Presumably Clynes had in mind the Government of Ireland Act, passed, then suspended, in 1914. But was this now to include the amendment on partition? And what of the wishes of the Irish majority who had rejected such Home Rule solutions by voting for Sinn Fein?

These questions were on the agenda at the conference of the reformed Second International in Berne in early 1919. To the chagrin of the Labour Party delegates, the Irish Labour Party were given seats as members of a party of a distinct and separate nation. Enough pressure was applied on the British delegates to persuade them to make a public declaration on their attitude to Ireland. This stressed:

> The British Labour Party has always supported Home Rule for Ireland, and is recognised by the Irish people as a steady and reliable ally in their agitation for national self-government. The subject has not only been dealt with in innumerable conferences, but in the election addresses of our candidates for parliament it invariably occupies a prominent position.[16]

The claims were exaggerated. Ireland had not been 'dealt with' in 'innumerable' debates, but once only; the Labour Party had not 'always supported Home Rule for Ireland', having only done so officially since 1913; and while the majority of election addresses had endorsed Home Rule, this was not the case for the majority of official election manifestos. There remained an ambiguity in the statement about what extent of Irish self-determination was acceptable to Labour. The Second International had no qualms, demanding in April 1919, that, 'The principle of free and absolute self-determination shall be applied immediately in the case of Ireland', and affirmed:

> the right of the Irish people to political independence; demands that this self-determination shall rest upon a democratic decision expressed by the free, equal and secret vote of the people, without any military, political or economic pressure from outside, or any reservation or restriction imposed by any government.[17]

The same month saw J.R. Clynes adopt a different tone in the House of Commons. During a debate on Ireland, he insisted his was the 'one party... which is united in the desire to meet the claims of Ireland embodied in the Act which was passed by such large majorities in this House'.[18]

This suggests that Clynes was still hankering after the 1914 Government of Ireland Act, which certainly did impose the type of 'restriction' on self-determination opposed by the Second International, and although Clynes admitted he was unable to 'go into the principles and certainly not the details of the special form of self-government which should be conceded to Ireland', he did stress, 'I am not arguing for independence'.[19]

The main thrust of the speech rested on the complaint that 'lawlessness and unconstitutional action have received every encouragement from the inaction of government', a reference, to both the pre-war antics of the Unionists and the unilateralism of Sinn Fein. It was, for Clynes, deplorable that the Nationalists who had 'stood for constitutional action and for law and order' were 'nearly destroyed at the polls', while Sinn Fein, 'which treats this country and this House with contempt and refused to come near it' had 'received the support of the great majority of the Irish people'. It was, said Labour's leader, the 'lawlessness' of Sinn Fein which was 'being especially encouraged by the government's neglect of this troublesome subject'.

'Troublesome' indeed. The choice of adjective spoke volumes

about the Labour Party's approach to Ireland: a wish to be rid of the whole bad business, but an unwillingness to attempt anything too drastic to secure the good riddance.

By mid-1919, the Labour Party was getting itself into a messy tangle on Ireland. It was still clinging nostalgically to the old Home Rule solution, unwilling to adopt the policy of the Second International of which it was a member, yet unable to canvass any precise solution of its own. In May that year Labour MPs V. Hartshorn and James Sexton, speaking in the House of Commons, attempted to develop a position. Hartshorn's contribution was illuminating, not for any suggestions he had on a policy for Ireland, but for his assessment of the political consequences if no solution was sought. His plea was for the House of Commons to rescue its own credibility and give force to the Labour Party's whole philosophy that peaceful reformism and constitutionalism worked:

> The Irish question is becoming more and more a labour question. It has become peculiarly a labour question because the Irish problem, in its effect, goes right down to the very roots of representative government and of parliamentary institutions. It would do well for this House to remember that parliamentary institutions are on trial before the workers of the world. They form a system that is being scrapped in several of the countries of Europe, a system that has not yet justified itself either in relation to the wrongs of Ireland or in relation to the wrongs of labour. I say with regret. I am not pleased to say it, I wish it were otherwise — organised workers are being slowly but surely forced to the conclusion that parliamentary government is a fraud.[20]

Hartshorn could be accused of making a universal mountain out of an Irish molehill. But the spring and summer of 1919 were difficult months for the leaders of the Labour Party and the trade unions. The discrediting of 'parliamentary institutions' in Ireland was one challenge. Another was the establishment of a Soviet government in Russia.

Even in Britain things were stirring. In February 1919 the miners union had voted for strike action as a means to securing nationalisation of the mines. In June, Labour's annual conference defeated the party leadership in endorsing a resolution which called for the 'unreserved use of their political and industrial power' to 'enforce their demands'.[21] Those stressing 'direct action' rather than waiting for the next general election for Labour to achieve its aims won similar victories at the TUC conference in September.

It all reflected a growth of militancy in the rank and file of the unions and the Labour Party, a militancy which questioned the reliance on parliamentary methods so prized by the party leadership. The issue of Ireland, though not central to this challenge, was part of it and was to become increasingly so in 1920.

Meanwhile the failure of Labour MPs to spell out their precise policy on Ireland continued. It was James Sexton who attempted clarification in the May 1919 parliamentary debate. His reference point was five questions put to the Labour Party in *The Times* on 13 May.

First was whether the Labour Party was in favour of the establishment of an Irish Republic and the complete separation of Ireland from Britain. Sexton was unequivocal:

> If I know the Labour Party at all — and from an association
> of over thirty years I think I ought to know it — I should say
> that the Labour Party was... very much opposed to the separa-
> tion of Ireland from the United Kingdom.[22]

Second was whether Labour supported 'Full dominion rule; that is, the right of the Irish government to maintain an army and navy, to enter into treaties with foreign powers'. Sexton affirmed that he was in favour of dominion rule but he maintained that such a form of separation did not involve 'the right to secede or to enter into treaties with foreign powers'.

Third was whether Labour was in favour of imposing a solution 'even if the majority of the Irish electorate refused to accept it'. Sexton argued: 'But this is not the case. The vast majority accepted the Home Rule Bill'.

Fourth Sexton took up the challenge of whether Ulster should be 'coerced', if the population there was opposed to the terms of a possible settlement. He answered that minorities had to accept the decision of majorities, but in reply to an interruption from Edward Carson, Sexton assured the Unionist leader: 'I have never heard that the Home Rule Act would drive any man out of the United Kingdom, and, if I thought that, I should vote against the Home Rule Bill.'

The final question was whether Labour would use the British Army against the Unionists. Sexton answered that, 'in Ireland now', British troops were employed 'not to coerce a minority, but to coerce a majority'. He also took the opportunity to define his attitude to Sinn Fein, saying that although that party were presently in a majority, 'I hope it will not last... I do not think it will last, because I think that the men who are following Sinn Fein today are following it because they are disgusted with political action and the action of this House towards Ireland.'

It was the most precise speech any Labour member had made in the Commons since the end of the war and the kindest comment which can be made on it is that it was naive. Ireland in 1919 was not the Ireland of 1912 when the Home Rule solution Sexton was still promoting was proposed in the Commons. It was no longer a question of a restricted form of Irish self-government, but whether Irish independence should be supported, and whether partition should be supported. Sexton and the Labour Party generally tried to shield their eyes from these realities, but this speech of May 1919 did give a clear reply to one of the relevant questions and half an answer to the other. Sexton's rejection of the 'separation of Ireland from the United Kingdom' was unambiguous. But, for all his criticism of giving in to the Unionist minority, his response to Carson implied that if this separation did occur, then as far as the British Labour Party was concerned, the right of the Unionists to opt out should be conceded. Sexton may not have spelled out an endorsement of partition, which he believed was unnecessary under the Home Rule solution. Nevertheless, the hint was there.

Although the Labour Party went on hoping that the dilemmas over independence and partition need not be faced, events in Ireland were again exposing their position as a flight from reality. The Irish Volunteers had killed two policemen escorting a cartload of gelignite in County Tipperary at the beginning of 1919. The rest of the year saw similar attacks carried out on the more accessible and identifiable representatives of British authority. The response of the British government was to send in more troops.

In December 1919 the Lloyd George government finally made its political intentions known. A new Government of Ireland Bill was presented to the Commons. It recommended two parliaments in Ireland, one for the six north-eastern counties, the other for the rest of the country. The powers of these parliaments were generally similar to those outlined in the 1912 Bill. Dail Eireann had been declared illegal three months earlier. There was to be no truck with independence.

The Labour Party, apart from its parliamentary wing, had had no opportunity to discuss these developments. After the excitement of 1918, the 1919 conference rolled back progress and did not discuss Ireland. However, judging from what Labour MPs had said prior to the introduction of the new Government of Ireland Bill, its proposals could only increase the Party's difficulties. On the one hand, the limits on Irish self-determination appeared to approximate Labour's own policy. On the other, the proposals on partition did not.

Consequently, by the end of 1919, the Irish controversy saw the following line-up: The British government saying it was against independence, for partition; the Irish majority had voted for independence, against partition; the British Labour Party, against independence, against partition. Labour's search was for the middle ground. The party didn't appear to notice that they were stranded in no-man's-land when it was time for the taking of sides.

4. The Policy Challenged

The British general election of 1918 had been the most successful in the Labour Party's existence. It polled 2.5 million votes compared to the 400,000 it had received in December 1910. Though it was rewarded with only 60 MPs, it secured 22 per cent of the vote. Moreover, the Liberal Party emerged from the election decimated and split, with most of its members following Lloyd George into the ruling coalition and the rest reduced to 26 seats under the leadership of Asquith.

The results held a strange element of paradox for Labour. Its rise mirrored the fall of the Liberals to whom it had, on most issues, including Ireland, been willing to serve as a political apprentice.

In parliament, the Irish Nationalists with their cherished memories of Charles Parnell and John Redmond were little more than a rump. Yet this party too had served for years as a model for Labour's pioneers. Now, both it and the Liberal Party had fallen on hard times and the Labour Party was left to carry on their traditions.

Since the days of Gladstone, the Liberals and the Irish Party had a common cause in Irish Home Rule. Labour in parliament had gone along with that, albeit in the most casual and cavalier fashion. But after 1918 circumstances demanded that they emerge from the disappearing shadows of the Liberals and the Redmondites in which they had sheltered for so long.

The publication of the 1920 Government of Ireland Bill gave the Labour Party the chance to come into its own. J.R. Clynes had kicked off on behalf of the Parliamentary Party during the second reading of the Bill by roundly condemning the proposed partition of Ireland:

Two parliaments, in the judgement of those for whom I speak, would inevitably create rival and separate interests, delaying rather than hastening the period... when there shall be a parliament speaking for Ireland...

My colleagues for whom I am speaking wish me to say that we oppose this scheme of self-government because it provides a form of partition founded on a religious basis and recognises neither the historic unity of the province of Ulster nor of Ireland as a whole.[1]

This was an unambiguous statement and more of the same was to follow. For the first time since the end of the war a spokesman for the Labour Party gave a detailed outline of party policy. Clynes continued:

There should be conceded to Ireland the maximum of self-government compatible with the unity of the Empire and the safety of the UK in time of war; the fullest financial and economic liberty, subject to an annual contribution towards the cost of expenditure which is common to us all... There should be adequate protection for the Ulster people from any sense of danger to their life, their property or their faith. There should be recognition of Ireland's right to discuss and decide in one elective assembly her own constitution and her own financial arrangements. These conditions... would literally amount to self-determination, limited only by the requirements of imperial unity and defence.[2]

Clynes ended with a rhetorical flourish: 'The remedy, as we believe, for the Irish trouble is to cease governing Ireland by force, not next month or next year, or after the Bill is passed, but to cease governing Ireland by force now.'[3]

The policy had been firmed up at a joint meeting of the Parliamentary Party and Labour's executive on 25 February. This endorsed a report based on an Ireland visit a month earlier by five Labour MPs led by Adamson and Henderson. The concept of a totally independent Ireland had now been formally rejected, in defiance of both the Second International and the Irish people voting in the 1918 election. But, the fudging of the previous two years had been superceded by a clear declaration of what was to be done to untangle 'this troublesome subject'. Ironically, having at last arrived at a policy, the party leadership was soon faced with a vigorous assault on it, and the most sustained internal debate on Ireland which the Labour Party had ever experienced.

Dissatisfaction with the qualifications Labour's leaders had placed on self-determination became evident as soon as the January 1920 report was drafted. The party's own *Daily Herald* commented:

> The delegation returned from their visit with a vivid realisation of the realities of the position of Ireland... they have realised that the only alternative to coercion lies not in the timorous and uneffective proposals for 'instalments of Home Rule' but in full and fearless application of the principle of self-determination... But it is a thousand pities that the delegates have, in one respect, swerved from adhesion to the principle they themselves have laid down. They suggest that in any negotiation it should be a pre-determined condition that defence and foreign relations should be 'reserved' to the imperial parliament. This is both illogical and impolitic. Self-determination of its very nature excludes such reservations.[4]

Towards the end of March a by-election in Stockport further posed the contradiction noted by the *Herald*. The Labour candidate was Sir Leo Chiozza Money, and both he and the party's national executive were quizzed by the electorate on their Irish policy. Money became immediately suspect because of the expression of an 'unsatisfactory attitude towards the shootings of Connolly and Pearse'.[5] The executive also failed to please when it met a two-man delegation representing the local Irish. Messrs Clancey and Lynch asked the executive to pledge Labour to a recognition of the Irish Republic, the withdrawal of the British Army from Ireland and the release of all political prisoners. The executive replied by issuing a long statement to the delegation and to the press. It quoted the Irish resolution adopted by the Labour party conference in June 1918, which limited the right to self-determination, and the statement from the 1919 Second International which did not. There was further equivocation in the rest of the statement:

> We believe that if Ireland were left free to decide whether she would remain within the Empire or become completely separated from it, the Irish themselves, upon mature consideration would decide that it was in their vital interest that the link should not be completely severed. But there is a vital distinction between Ireland remaining part of the United Kingdom under compulsion and remaining as a result of her own choice. Whatever form of union may be maintained should be arranged by agreement... It must be recognised that

an immediate decision on the issue of the Union or Separation might not be a true reflex of the considered opinion of the majority of the Irish people. The present atmosphere is neither healthy nor normal... These factors are calculated to prejudice any attempt to ascertain the considered and mature opinion of the majority of the Irish people on the issue of Union or Separation and they might result in the sacrificing of Ireland's ultimate interests to the immediate satisfaction that might be gained by a total repudiation of any form of connection with their old-time political oppressors. The first essential is to change the attitude of people due to generations of unavailing struggle for freedom.[6]

These lengthy deliberations neither impressed nor satisfied the Stockport Irish. They put up William O'Brien, secretary of the Irish Labour Party and Trade Union Congress, and a political prisoner, in the by-election. O'Brien received 2,336 votes. Labour lost the election by just over 6,000. Although the result indicates that Labour would have lost with or without the Irish intervention, O'Brien's candidature was a worrying development for the party. If repeated elsewhere, tens of thousands of votes could be lost. Equally ominous was that someone as prominent as O'Brien in the Irish labour movement had been put up to challenge the British Labour Party's candidate. The executive of the Irish Labour Party and TUC publically disassociated itself from the O'Brien campaign, but it did agree that the ploy was 'an effective piece of propaganda work'.[7] Adding to the tensions, the Irish party had the previous year encouraged 'disaffected Irish workers' in Britain to 'organise themselves in groups, [to] bring all their influence to bear upon the national and local labour organisation to Britain', so to 'force their British fellow-workers to face boldly the implications of their professed love of liberty and their doctrine of self-determination'.[8]

Under such pressure, and no doubt with the lessons of Stockport in mind, the leaders of the British Labour Party attempted to mend some of the fences. The party had already rejected a demand for affiliation from the Belfast Labour Party in 1919, recognising that its proper place was with the Irish party, and they now used the opportunity of the Government of Ireland Bill to canvass the Irish as to what strategy British Labour should adopt in parliament towards that legislation.

The advice offered was reported to the House of Commons by J.R. Clynes on 18 May, when the Bill was at committee stage. Discussing the section which proposed partition, Clynes said:

> Hon. Members with whom I am associated have decided... to vote against this Clause and throughout the remaining stages take no part whatever in the progress of the Bill... The Irish Labour Party and Trades Union Congress have sent us a communication in which they say: 'The Labour Party's best policy is to ignore it (the Bill) as we shall probably do if it became an Act of Parliament'.[9]

This was an exceptional step for the Parliamentary Labour Party, amounting almost to abstentionism, the very policy of the much-criticised Sinn Fein. After a number of contributions to this particular committee stage, Labour did indeed withdraw, to return during the Third Reading.

One contribution hinted at the pressure the Labour Party was feeling from the Irish in Britain: 'In this country those who are identified with the working class movement in districts where Irishmen form a considerable portion of the industrial population are absolutely opposed to this Bill'.[10] The clearest statement came from Neil Maclean, Glasgow MP and expelled member of the revolutionary Socialist Labour Party which had been established with the help of James Connolly: 'We want Ireland one and undivided; Ireland without partition, to have the right to say that Ireland shall govern itself with its own parliament according to the wishes and desires of all the Irish people.'[11]

All of which suggests a sudden bellicosity in Labour's Irish policy. But that is only part of the picture. In the same month that the Ireland Bill was boycotted and Labour MPs were stating their total hostility to partition, the Labour Party produced a pamphlet which had a rather different tone. The pamphlet, *Irish Nationalism and Labour Internationalism*, had a forward by Clynes and was written by George Bernard Shaw. Not the Shaw who had protested at the 1916 executions, but Shaw the Fabian.

It began by insisting that Labour, 'is not and by its own nature can never be a separatist party: it is a federalist party, and, far from wishing to detach the Irish people from the English, it aims at establishing the closest possible relations between both'.[12]

The rest of the pamphlet was a mixture of early Fabianism

and pre-1912 Labourism. There was a call for Home Rule parliaments for Scotland, Ireland and England, an assertion that 'Life is harder in England than Ireland', and a wish to be rid of the whole controversy on the grounds that: 'When the Irish worker sees in the English worker his fellow sufferer and comrade, the Irish question will finally escape from the romantic stage to the practical one, and cease to be a mere excuse for British capitalist statesmen to neglect British affairs.'

There were dangers in Shaw's eccentricities. For example:

> Partition, however, may easily become an abusive name for quite beneficial measures of decentralisation and local autonomy. Though there is nothing favourable to be said for a political division of Ireland into Catholics and Protestants, it is not clear to Englishmen that there is any radical objection into federated provinces... the Labour Party regards the question as open.[13]

This was hardly the same emphasis that Neil Maclean placed on Labour's opposition to partition, but there was one issue on which Shaw did not prevaricate. This was what he termed the 'military question', the answer to which was:

> It is impossible to treat Ireland as a separate country from Great Britain for military purposes. An invasion of Ireland would be an invasion of Britain... the Labour Party earnestly desires that the two islands should form a single unit for military purposes.[14]

Historians could be tempted to treat Shaw's pamphlet as primarily of scholarly relevance. Yet it was produced officially by the Labour Party and its foreword by J.R. Clynes, one of the leading Labour MPs, did claim: 'The weight of common sense to be found in these pages reflects the position which the Labour Party has tried to maintain with regard to Ireland'. Most important, Clynes singled out Shaw's remarks on the 'military question' as being something which 'Irishmen... can turn to with great profit'.

While these words, and the pamphlet which contained them, were circulating in Britain, the population of Ireland was facing a 'military question' of a different nature. This was the British escalation of the Anglo-Irish war; for a war it had now become. The escalation took several forms. One was a system of 'reprisals' where the British attempted to 'punish' Sinn Feiners, or, at times, the Irish population generally, for the successes of the Irish Republican Army, as the Republican fighters were now known. The most infamous act in the first six months of 1920 was the murder of Tomas MacCurtan, Lord Mayor of Cork and Commandant of Cork No. 1 Brigade of the IRA. MacCurtan was killed in his own home by a band of masked raiders, who have always been suspected to have been members of the Irish police.

It was not so much the police, but those who came to assist them who symbolised the new and deadly coercion. These were the 'Black and Tans', so called because of the colour of their uniforms, who were sent to Ireland in March 1920, and the Auxiliary Division, who began their operations in July. Consisting, respectively, of demobilised soldiers from the ranks of the British Army and ex-Army officers, these forces spearheaded the government's search for a military solution. Their methods were those used to put down colonial rebellions — reprisals, intimidation of the community, murder and looting. Ireland, however, was not an obscure dot on a map of faraway Africa and it was not acceptable to see its people as pagans with dark skins. Consequently, while the government's use of terrror was, from its point of view, the only available military reply to the national revolution it was facing in Ireland, it was too close to home to be easily explained to the British public.

There were signs that this public was beginning to take notice. In the spring and summer of 1920, the Socialist Labour Party took the Irish revolutionary Sean McLoughlin around Britain. He addressed large and enthusiastic audiences, with as many as 20,000 people attending the nine meetings in Yorkshire.[15] His message was for recognition of the Irish Republic, and such propaganda was having its effect within the Labour Party itself. In April 1920 the annual conference of the Independent Labour Party, to which many of the leading personalities in the Labour Party still belonged, passed a resolution which 'welcomed' the formation of the Irish Republic.[16] Around the same time Arthur Henderson was reported as declaring that he favoured 'Irish self-determination without qualification or reservation'.[17]

These events reflected the growing crisis over British policy in Ireland. They suggested too that the rank and file of the Labour Party were beginning to take an interest in Ireland. The resolutions to the annual party conference in June 1920 were evidence of these stirrings. Of the three dealing with Ireland, those from the Marylebone and East Hants parties asserted the right to Irish self-determination. They added the 'hope' that the Irish would choose to stay in the British Empire, but added 'the final decision must rest' with the Irish. An amendment deleting the section that hoped Ireland stayed in Empire was submitted from the British Socialist Party.[18]

These resolutions, on top of the mounting external pressures, suggested the party leadership at the 1920 conference would not easily escape with the type of ambiguous resolution that had been passed two years earlier. Nevertheless, such a ploy was attempted, in the form of a long resolution put forward by the party executive. It started boldly, declaring that 'the time has passed for half measures and any more shilly-shallying'. It suggested:

> The conference reaffirms the resolution adopted by the Permanent Commission of the International at Amsterdam in April 1919, demanding that the principle of free and absolute self-determination shall be applied immediately in the case of Ireland.

To implement such a policy the resolution called for the election of an all-Ireland constituent assembly, the 'withdrawal of the British Army of Occupation' and 'the handing over of the transitional adminstration to the leaders of the majority of the Irish people'. Finally, there was a demand that the British government accept any constitution drawn up by the proposed constituent assembly. On this last point there was, however, a qualification: such a constitution could only be accepted provided it dealt with 'exclusively Irish affairs'.[19]

This was the same limitation which had been agreed two years earlier: the brick wall of George Bernard Shaw's 'military question', where Irish self-determination could be supported only in so far as Britain's 'security' was not threatened.

Even before Sidney Webb, a Fabian like Shaw, moved the resolution on behalf of the party executive there were protests. On a point of order a delegate from the floor of the conference moved that the resolution be referred back to the executive for redrafting , on the grounds that it was 'contradictory'.[20] Another delegate supported the objection and called for a vote on the referral back, but the conference chairman rejected the request. When Webb finally rose to speak it became apparent that the debate was going to centre on the phrase 'exclusively Irish affairs', for the bulk of his speech was given over to a defence of this formulation. Webb's comments were reported as follows:

> Self-determination for Ireland did not mean that they wished the Irish to interfere with the affairs of Great Britain. Therefore, when they said they wished to give Ireland self-determination for its own affairs he thought they should go on to say they hoped Ireland will come together with them again and talk over what was necessarily their common affairs, and so shape the relations between the two countries that they might get the greatest measure of liberty for each... Therefore, whilst they might be quite frank and sincere in offering Ireland complete self-determination for all Irish affairs they did not mean they wanted Ireland to go spinning along the road like a motor hog without regard to anyone else on the road.[21]

The first two speakers who followed Webb spoke more generally on the worthiness of self-determination, but the next two, J. Walker from the Iron and Steel Trades and R.J. Davis from Salford West Labour Party repeated the call for reference back. Walker did so because he wanted it emphasised that the Labour Party was 'not prepared to vote for an Irish Republic', while Davis argued for unequivocal support for the Republic.

This double attack, from the right and left, on what was termed the 'vagueness of the resolution' was sufficient to carry the conference which proceeded to vote for a redrafting.

When the resolution came back the phrase 'exclusively Irish affairs' had been dropped, a victory for the pro-Republicans. When Sidney Webb moved the motion for the second time he did his best to dissociate the party executive from it, explaining it was his 'duty' to submit the motion, and if 'some delegates did not find the resolution all to their liking the fault... was not with the executive'.[22]

After the motion had been seconded, Walker from the Iron and Steel Trades rose for the second time. He proposed an amendment which reinserted, 'exclusively Irish affairs', and added a further limitation — that any Irish parliament had to be 'within the British Commonwealth'. He argued that 'the people of Ulster did not want separation' and that 'Ireland, England,

Scotland and Wales were inevitably, irrevocably bound
together, and we in this country needed the help of Ireland just
as much as Ireland just as much as Ireland needed our help'.[23]

Walker was answered by ILP delegate Emanuel Shinwell,
who called on the conference to 'make up its mind on the simple
issue — where they in favour of giving to the Irish people a form
of government best suited to themselves, or were they going to
put their foot down on the attempt of the Irish people to decide
their own destiny?'. Shinwell called for unfettered self-
determination. He was opposed by a trade union delegate from
Belfast who argued against any form of Irish self-rule, saying he
wanted 'Ireland back in its place amongst the four nations which
composed these islands'. He went on to allege that 'the Sinn Fein
movement... was an octopus composed of gombeen men, the
publicans and gin-sellers'.

The next speaker was T. Cunningham from Ardwick (Manchester) Labour Party. Backing the resolution and opposing the
amendment, he referred to the damage the 'lack of unity on the
part of the party on the Irish question' was doing to Labour.
This 'difficulty', said Cunningham, 'had left us with a legacy
that was preventing us from getting at the real task and getting
the Irish people on the Labour side as they ought to have been all
the time'.[24]

J.H. Thomas addressed the conference in a final attempt to
swing the delegates behind the amendment. 'It was idle to deny
there was an Ulster problem,' said Thomas. He insisted: 'the
Labour movement would not agree to the establishment of an
Irish Republic'.

Finally, Ben Tillett of the dockers' union was called on to
speak. Tillett was, by now, one of the elder statesmen of the
Labour Party. He had been a leader of the great dock strike of
1889, one of the first struggles of the 'new unionism' which had
sought to organise and turn militant the unskilled or semi-skilled
workers. He had always been on the left of the party. In 1908 he
had published a pamphlet, *Is the Parliamentary Party a Failure?*,
denouncing the parliamentary leaders as 'sheer hypocrites' guilty
of 'gross betrayal of the class that willingly supports them'.[25] But
on the Irish issue his record was more patchy, having criticised
Sinn Fein at the 1918 annual conference of the TUC.

Such sentiments were absent in his speech to the 1920

Labour conference, in which Tillett argued that as a consequence of past attitudes of the Labour Party, 'the Irish nation, the Irish democracy, the Irish industrial classes, had as great a suspicion of the Labour Party conference as they had of the Coalition government'.[26] For such suspicions to be confounded, 'the conference should give absolute freedom to the Irish people'.

Whether this contribution from such a respected figure as Tillett was crucial in swaying the delegates is hard to say, but when the vote was taken the supporters of 'absolute freedom' secured a narrow victory. The amendment proposed by Walker and supported by the party leadership was defeated by 1,191,000 votes to 945,000. The main resolution was then easily carried. It had been the most thorough discussion the Labour Party had ever held on Ireland and resulted in the first defeat the party leadership had ever suffered on the issue. For the first time the British Labour Party had given unconditional support to Irish self-determination.

As is the way with radical resolutions passed at conferences of the Labour Party, the policy was not to be reflected in the activities and words of the party leaders. The following month, speaking in the Commons, J.H. Thomas limited demands to 'Dominion Home Rule'. Nevertheless, the 1920 conference decision reflected the strength of feeling now building up in the ranks of the Labour Party. It seems likely that it was the votes of the local party delegates to the annual conference, rather than those of the affiliated unions which secured the defeat of the Walker amendment. The evidence is not just the fact that Tillett was the only trade union delegate to speak against the amendment, but that when a similar debate took place at a special conference of the TUC a month later a proposal to substitute an endorsement of 'Dominion Home Rule' with a demand for 'recognition... and immediate application of the right of the Irish people to determine the form of government they desire' was defeated by a large majority.[27]

Yet even the TUC conference adopted a resolution calling for the withdrawal of the British Army and its auxiliaries from Ireland. More surprisingly, this motion stated: 'We recommend a general down-tools policy and call on the trade unions here represented to carry out this policy, each according to its own constitution, by taking a ballot of its members or otherwise'.[28]

Although this amounted to the advocation of a general strike in Britain it was not so revolutionary as it seems. It was essentially an exercise in buck passing. The idea of the general strike was agreed, but because the implementation of such a course of action was passed on to the individual unions the TUC leaders were fully aware it was never likely to happen.

Nevertheless the passing of such a resolution indicated the pressure the leaders of the labour movement were under to do something positive about Ireland. Later in the year the leaders of the party and the TUC faced the most widespread and militant campaign that had ever been mounted among the British working class on the Irish issue.

The National Council of Action was formed on 9 August 1920 from representatives of the TUC, the Labour Party executive and the Parliamentary Labour Party. It was established to 'use all the resources at the disposal of Labour to prevent the British nation being plunged into war, and by all means open to them to restore peace to the world'.

Specifically, the Council was set up to mobilise the labour movement against possible British intervention in the Soviet-Polish War. However, by the time the formation of the Council of Action was endorsed at a thousand-strong delegate meeting on 13 August, British premier Lloyd George had already withdrawn his previous threats to march against the Soviet Union.

Since some 350 local Councils of Action had already been established across the country, many of them decided to concentrate their attention not on a war which could happen but on one which was going on. An early example was a resolution sent by Hendon Council of Action to the national council on 7 September, calling on them to 'extend their terms of reference to the unofficial war with Ireland'.[29]

The call was repeated in various forms by more than seventy local councils and Labour Parties over the following four months. A number of examples can be given which give a taste of the general flavour of the demands. West Ham Trades Council and Central Labour Party wanted 'swift action to end the present state of affairs in Ireland'.[30] Waterloo branch of the Liverpool Labour Party warned that if the Council of Action failed to act on Ireland, 'it will be detrimental to the interests of the party in this locality'.[31] Willesden Council of Action demanded a national conference to discuss 'immediate action' on the Soviet-Polish War, unemployment and Ireland.[32] The local council in Newcastle-under-Lyme called for 'strike action to end the Anglo-Irish war',[33] while Partington Labour Party in Manchester called on the national council to raise the issue of Ireland 'before the assembly of the League of Nations'.[34]

At first, the joint secretaries of the national council replied to these demands politely, explaining that the 'Council's mandate is strictly limited to Russia'.[35] But the more the calls for action poured in, the less courteous the replies became. When, in late November, Methil District Council of Action called for the 'forceable take-over by Councils of Action of all factories' if British troops weren't immediately withdrawn from Ireland,[36] the joint secretary rather pointedly replied: 'It is one thing to get the resolution in the terms you enclose adopted at a meeting of your local Council of Action, but I should like to know what are the views of the individual members of your branch'.[37]

Eventually, on discovering that the Birmingham and Northeast district Councils of Action had been circulating a model resolution on Ireland, the national joint secretary decided a conspiracy was afoot. In a letter dated 12 January 1921 he noted the Birmingham model resolution and complained that because the 'majority of councils' endorsed the Birmingham motion:

> The result has been that we had to spend hours of our time explaining to local councils... that the mandate conferred upon us... was a limited one... Frankly, we have too much work to do to deal with sort of organised misapprehension.[38]

This was an over reaction given the mildness of the model resolution which stated:

> That we strongly urge that a national conference be held to consider the strengthening of the national council and the extension of their scope to stop the war in Ireland as was done in regards to the Polish-Russian war.[39]

Most of the resolutions sent in went much further, only a few of them used the exact wording. Certainly, the circulation of the resolution may have prompted the local councils and Labour Parties to call for action on Ireland, but such was the quantity of resolutions submitted that it is fair to surmise that the feeling

was already there. Indeed, it was not only labour movement
bodies who called upon the labour leaders to act. An editorial in
the *Manchester Guardian* of 22 September 1920 advised the
trade unions to use 'direct action to paralyse all repressive
government action in Ireland', while on 3 December a telegram
sent to the party leadership read: 'New Zealand Labour Party
urges Council of Action to do something to help Ireland'.[40] It
was signed by the president, vice-president and secretary of the
New Zealand party. Other indications of the growth of popular
protest at the government's Irish policy include the success of
The Irish Tragedy: Scotland's Disgrace written by the Scottish
revolutionary John MacLean. This forthright condemnation of
British policy sold 20,000 copies in Scotland alone during the
autumn of 1920.[41] MacLean spoke of Britain's 'brutal treatment
of Ireland, more blatant today than ever before'.

The contemporary situation in Ireland provides one explanation for the mounting protests. In the North, anti-Catholic riots
in Belfast and Derry during May, June and July drove hundreds
of Catholics and some Protestant socialists from their work-
places. In September, the government appeared to encourage
such pogroms when it endorsed Unionist plans to form a Special
Constabulary and a Special Reserve Constabulary. This
amounted to arming the Northern Loyalists, since the Reserves,
who were to become the 'B' Specials, were formed from the
ranks of the Ulster Volunteers who had been threatening
rebellion against the British parliament six years earlier.

For the South, the British government had passed the
'Restoration of Order in Ireland Act' on 9 August, giving the
military in Ireland the right to intern without charge or trial, the
power to try by court martial, and the right to suspend coroners'
inquests into violent deaths. On 10 December, Cork, Tipperary,
Kerry and Limerick were placed under martial law. The following evening Auxiliaries and Black and Tans burned, looted and
destroyed the centre of Cork as a reprisal for an IRA attack on
Auxiliaries two days earlier.

All this took place at a time when the Labour movement in
Britain was particularly receptive to organising support for the
Irish majority. The first world war and the Russian revolution
had helped commit the labour movement to internationalism.
Between 1918 and 1921 a new militancy and confidence swept

the British working class. Membership of trade unions rose dramatically. So did the sales of left wing papers. On the wages front, the dockers and railway workers won important victories in 1920. The widespread belief that the threat of a general strike had prevented British involvement in the Soviet-Polish war seemed another good argument for the labour movement adopting direct action in support of the Irish cause.

For the parliamentary leaders of the Labour Party such a course was unthinkable. It was foreign to their whole constitutional methodology. When the third reading of the Government of Ireland Bill was heard in the Commons in November 1920, the Parliamentary Labour Party met and adopted the following approach:

> That the British Army of Occupation should be withdrawn; that the question of Irish government should be relegated to a constituent assembly, elected on the basis of proportional representation, and that the constitution drawn up by the constituent assembly should be accepted, provided it afforded protection to the minority and would prevent Ireland becoming a military or naval menace to Great Britain.[42]

This was not the policy approved by the party conference a few months earlier. It contained the same general limitations placed on Irish self-determination which had been part of the defeated Walker amendment. However, by November 1920 the party leadership had, for the first time managed to win the support of the leadership of the Irish labour movement for conditional self-determination.

This process had begun in September when the executive of the Labour Party invited a delegation from the Irish Trades Union Congress and Labour Party to visit London to try to agree a common policy. When four representatives of Irish labour met the Labour Party executive, as well as the Parliamentary Committee of the TUC and the PLP on 18 October, their initial reaction was one of scepticism. They had been 'generally satisfied' with the policy agreed at the June conference, but 'noted with concern that within a fortnight of the conference some Labour Members of Parliament were advocating a policy that fell short of' the conference decision.[43]

Arthur Henderson, on behalf of the party executive, parried these criticisms by suggesting the establishment of a joint consultative committee of the Irish and British movements.

Within a month the British party had won over their Irish
counterparts. At a special congress of the Irish TUCLP on 10
November a motion was agreed accepting the two restrictions on
self-determination which were to appear shortly afterwards in
the PLP statement on the third reading of the Government of
Ireland Bill: protection for the minority and the 'military or
naval menace' question. In return for these concessions Henderson agreed to send a Labour Party delegation to Ireland at the
end of the year.

It was this policy that was outlined by Adamson during the
third reading of the Government of Ireland Bill. Adamson
acknowledged that 'the great bulk of the Irish people in the
south and west are, undoubtedly, demanding complete independence', but he argued that this demand was a passing fancy:
'I do not believe in their heart of hearts they really want a
republic; they are simply putting forward, in my opinion, their
maximum demand.'[44] And, whatever the Irish people wanted,
Adamson continued, 'the Labour Party do not believe in an
Irish Republic. The Labour Party do not want to see an Irish
Republic established'. But what if the Irish disregard the wishes
of the British Labour Party?

> We believe that the Irish people should be given the right to
> determine for themselves and, if you give them that right, you
> give them perfect freedom of choice. I am sure that it is not
> beyond the wisdom of the government to devise ways and
> means for producing an atmosphere which will bring out the
> best in the Irish people and induce them to give an expression
> of kinship with us.[45]

Adamson ended by outlining the details of the policy that had
been agreed at the meeting of the PLP.

What is perhaps most interesting is Adamson's reference to
the establishment of an Irish Republic as a 'maximum demand'.
This is reminiscent of the kind of trade union mentality
displayed by the majority of Labour MPs at the time. Most of
them had been trade union officials and they advocated the same
negotiation procedures over the Irish situation of 1920 as were,
and are, used to dealing with wage claims: there is a maximum
demand, a minimum offer and good sense that arrives at a compromise. That was exactly the approach the British government
adopted one year later — the consequences of which confirm that

there is neither peace nor satisfaction in a halfway house solution to the question of national self-determination.

Meanwhile, the Labour leaders were still facing demands for action rather than statements in the House of Commons. One response was the appointment of the 'Commission of Inquiry' Henderson had promised the Irish TUCLP. It was composed of representatives from the three sectors of the British labour movement as well as Tom Johnson from the Irish Labour Party and TUC.

The commission visited Ireland in December and met representatives of Sinn Fein, the labour movement and the Irish churches, as well as the Unionists.

Their report produced no surprises. It strongly condemned the actions of the British military and proposed a solution in line with the policy statement of the PLP the previous month. In addition, there was an appeal for a ceasefire which was ignored by the British government.

The commission's report became the basis of the Labour Party's first public campaign on the Irish issue. It was initiated on 29 December at a special party conference attended by 800 delegates. The main resolution, from the party executive, began with a condemnation of the 'outrages conducted in the name of Sinn Fein and reprisals by servants of the Crown'. What followed was in line with the by then unanimous opinion of the PLP, the commission and the Irish labour movement. It called for 'withdrawal of all armed forces... the responsibility for maintaining order in each locality in Ireland on the local authorities' and:

> an immediate election, by proportional representation of an entirely open constitutional assembly, charged to work out, at the earliest possible moment, without limitation or fetters, whatever constitution for Ireland and Irish people desire, subject to only two conditions, that it affords protection to minorities, and that the constitution should prevent Ireland from becoming a military or naval menace to Great Britain.[46]

When the resolution was presented to the delegates, the party leadership ensured there would be no repeat of the June conference dissent. No amendment to the resolution was allowed.[47] There was no way in which delegates could formally move the Councils of Action calls for strike action to secure British withdrawal. Neither was there any mechanism to deal with the obvious contradiction in the resolution: the call for an Irish constitution 'without limitation or fetters' and the placing of two conditions for acceptance by Britain.

When a delegate from Richmond Labour Party asked why the section concerning 'military or naval menace' had to be included, she was told by the conference chairman that it was 'to meet public superstition and prejudice'.[48]

Not surprisingly, the resolution was overwhelmingly accepted. Over the following months the Labour Party held more than 500 public meetings to explain its policy and produced tens of thousands of leaflets calling for 'Peace with Ireland'.

Compared with what the party had done previously this was an impressive level of activity. It was described by the *New Statesman* as 'one of the most successful campaigns' the Labour Party had ever mounted.[49]

Yet, it can be asked, how much was this chain of events — the commission, the special conference and the public meetings — a rather pale substitute for the course demanded of the Labour Party from the Councils of Action right through to the *Manchester Guardian*?

Certainly the proposed policy was less radical than that agreed at the June annual conference and the action taken in pursuit of it much less dramatic than that threatened over possible British intervention in the Soviet-Polish War.

When criticisms were made of the party leaders they retorted by blaming their membership, and the public at large. 'Bad as the situation is,' wrote Clynes in February 1921, 'public opinion is not prepared for a settlement of the Irish troubles by means of strikes'.[50] On another occasion J.H. Thomas explained that he was opposed to a strike in sympathy with the Irish, 'not because he didn't understand their position, nor because he didn't approve of their opinions, but because we knew that not five per cent of the men would strike in England on that issue'.[51]

Neither Clynes nor Thomas would have been likely to favour strike action even if it could have been proved that the whole of the British labour movement was keen to down tools — their politics did not encourage such tactics. That doesn't necessarily mean they were wrong in their assessment of British working class opinion. The rank and file of the Labour Party had been very slow to offer any response to the Irish solution. What made the militancy of the Councils of Action so dramatic was that nothing like it had been seen before. By the end of 1920, the more politically conscious sections of the working class believed a general strike over the government's Irish policy was possible. This confidence was not confined to the marxist or syndicalist groups outside the Labour Party — even the ILP submitted a resolution to the Labour Party's 1921 conference calling for a general strike on Ireland.[52] Three local parties also submitted resolutions to this conference on the same lines, and ten other resolutions or amendments on Ireland submitted were to the left of the executive's position. This was the highest number of motions on Ireland ever submitted to a Labour conference up to that time.

At the conference only the executive resolution was debated.

There was the occasional complaint that the motion was 'pious' and 'too mild', but, the Labour leaders again made great play of the fact that its policy was shared by the Irish Labour Party and TUC.

By June 1921, the general militancy that had been evident in the ranks of the labour movement twelve months before was no longer there. In 1920 the aggregate number of working days lost in strikes was 85,872,200. In 1921 it was 19,850,000. The reasons for this dramatic fall need not be elaborated. Suffice it to say that accelerating unemployment and an economic recession demobilised the working class, compounded by the collapse of the Triple Alliance of miners, railway and transport workers in April 1921 when, on 'Black Friday', the union leaders called off a solidarity strike in support of the miners. By mid-1921 the leaders of the Labour Party and the unions had seen off the challenge from the left, whether it be on direct action, nationalisation of the mines or on Ireland.

This meant that when negotiations with the Irish began in June 1921, the British government was under no pressure from the Labour Party to concede Sinn Fein's demands. Indeed when the Anglo-Irish peace conference began on 11 October and became the target of right wing critics of the government in the House of Commons, Arthur Henderson assured Lloyd George that while 'we are still opposed to the policy which the govern-

ment has followed during the last two to three years' the Labour
Party 'will give the government our unqualified support until
they have had a fair opportunity of carrying the conference
through to a successful conclusion'.

However, he added:

> No permanent scheme which divides Ireland into two parts
> will ever secure the approval of the majority of the Irish
> people... we shall examine the findings of the conference and
> apply certain tests:
> 1) Whether the proposals satisfy the majority of the Irish
> people... 2) there must be some form of protection for the
> minority... 3) we shall examine the proposal from the stand-
> point of the security of our country.[53]

The Anglo-Irish negotiations continued until the early
hours of 6 December when the Articles of Agreement were finally
signed by the Irish representatives. It was, Lloyd George was to
say, 'the greatest day in the history of the British Empire',[54] an
exaggeration, but indicative of the sense of triumph on the
British side. The Irish Republic, proclaimed in 1916 and given a
reality after the 1918 elections, was no more. In its place was a
partitioned Ireland. Both parts remained in the Empire, with the
North staying in the Union through its rights to send MPs to
Westminster. Britain was given the right to maintain a naval
presence in five Irish ports, and the Southern parliament was
obliged to swear an oath of allegiance to the British monarchy.
The possibility of eventual Irish unity was suggested in the
proposal to form a Council of Ireland, while the definitive boundaries of the two states was left to a border commission.

Lloyd George had secured the agreement of the Irish
negotiators through skilled diplomacy, false promises, lies, and,
in the end, a threat of 'total war' if the Irish refused to sign. The
president of the now doomed Republic, Eamon de Valera had
taken no part in the final negotiations in the hope that by staying
in Ireland he would make it impossible for his representatives to
sign any agreement without referring it back to Dublin. He was
wrong, and he and the people of Ireland were to pay a heavy
price for that mistake. In the South of Ireland a civil war would
be fought over the terms of the Treaty; in the North, the
Unionist state was given structures that would guarantee permanent conflict.

An informed observer of Ireland could have guessed that the Treaty was by no means the end of the business. It established the partition of Ireland which the Labour Party had so strongly opposed in May 1920 and forced the parliamentary party to boycott the Government of Ireland Bill in protest. The Treaty was in opposition to the position of the Second International of April 1919 which had insisted upon 'free and absolute self-determination'. It made no provision for a 32-county constituent assembly, one of the main planks of Labour policy for nearly a year, and there was no proof it could 'satisfy the majority of the Irish people' as demanded by Henderson in October 1920.

And yet, Labour leaders in parliament welcomed the Treaty in the Commons debate. The speech of Clynes gives the flavour:

> These articles in themselves I regard as a triumph of national patriotism, a victory for enduring national spirit over every obstacle and every form of force... Reference has been made to the attitude of the Labour Party in relation to these articles. These Articles travel on the lines advocated by Labour... I will only add that on the whole history of this Irish problem, and especially in relation to the stage which has now been reached, the conscience of the Labour Party is easy. I am, however, less concerned to try to apportion any degree of praise or blame for the stage which has now been reached than to make a contribution to party unity which alone finally secures a settlement and will put the seal to a finish of these unhappy quarrels between Ireland and this country... I look upon these Articles of Agreement as the instrument of a lasting and beneficent settlement between Ireland and this country...
>
> I say, therefore, that the Labour Party rejoices with those who, either in this House or in the country welcome this Agreement. We are eager to approve it, and are convinced it has the support of the vast majority of the Irish people. We are convinced that, if the people of both the North and the South of Ireland will try it, they will find, in the real test of it, that prosperity, that happiness and contentment for their country, which in days of conflict they have never been able to find.[55]

A later speech by Arthur Henderson hailed the Treaty as 'an honourable peace' which would 'open up a new era of friendship and mutual confidence between the British and Irish peoples'.[56] The decades which followed have given their own verdict on the Anglo-Irish Treaty and no words could offer a more cruel judgement on Clyne's and Henderson's complacent smugness.

One observation can be added. It had been 21 years and ten months since the Labour Party had been formed, as the Labour Representation Committee. In terms of the British patriotism, the imperial trappings, the search for compromise, the rhetoric, the conservatism and the self-righteousness associated with the House of Commons, it was indeed the case that in December 1921 the British Labour Party had come of age.

5. Making Partition Concrete

The little the 1921 Treaty gave Irish Republicans had not been achieved cheaply. Many were killed in the struggle for independence and even more were to die in the civil war which was fought in the South of Ireland over the terms of the Treaty.

One of the most famous casualties of the Anglo-Irish conflict was Terence McSweeney, the Lord Mayor of Cork who died after 73 days on hunger strike in Brixton prison. McSweeney had been arrested and tried before a military court before being transferred to the London jail.

His arrest and treatment was strongly condemned by the British labour movement. On 30 August 1920 the Prime Minister Lloyd George received a telegram:

> The whole of organised British labour asks you to reconsider the government's decision to allow the Lord Mayor of Cork to die rather than release him. His suffering greater than lengthy imprisonment. His death will make Irish solution more remote. Appeal to you to do the big thing.[1]

The telegram was signed by all the leading figures in the Labour Party and TUC, including William Adamson, chairman of the Parliamentary Labour Party, Arthur Henderson, secretary of the Labour Party and J.H. Thomas, chairman of the parliamentary committee of the TUC.

They were not alone in demanding McSweeney's release. A number of Liberal MPs made similar appeals. Among them was William Benn.

On 20 August 1920 he demanded to know from the Prime Minister: 'For what offence the Lord Mayor has been arrested, what is his present state of health and when will he be brought to public trial?'[2] McSweeney was never brought to public trial and died in Brixton prison. The massive funeral procession through London included prominent Labour Party leaders.

The Anglo-Irish Treaty was designed to end all such controversies. It did not, and in 1924 when a minority Labour government came to power it was immediately faced with the 'Irish question' — in the form of a problem over the Boundary Commission promised in the Anglo-Irish Treaty.

The Commission's purpose was to establish the frontier between the North and South. During the Treaty negotiations the Southern Irish (then the Irish Free State, later Eire and eventually the Republic of Ireland) had been led to believe that they would be awarded a good deal of extra territory. Knowing this, the Unionists in the North consistently blocked the establishment of the Commission.

When Ramsay MacDonald became Labour's first Prime Minister the Unionists were still stonewalling. MacDonald had little inclination to press the Unionists and when the Southern Irish government complained, he told them: 'Very serious trouble would be created in Ulster' if the Commission was established.[3]

The Southern government then tried a bluff of its own. The President of the Irish Free State, William Cosgrave, told MacDonald that if the Commission wasn't set up then the Southern parliament, 'would become a revolutionary parliament and the issue of an Irish Republic would come to be heard'.[4] This was enough to persuade MacDonald to fulfil the Treaty obligation. The Boundary Commission was duly established, although eventually its members failed to agree and the border stayed where it had been temporarily located in 1921.

The constitutional relationship between Britain and the South of Ireland came to the fore in 1931 when MacDonald was again Prime Minister, this time not in a Labour administration but in the National government which he had split the Labour Party to form.

J.H. Thomas was also in this government as Secretary of State for the Dominions. Since the Irish Free State was deemed to be a 'dominion' of Britain, it was Thomas who was mainly involved, on the British side, in the row which erupted in 1932.

The clash was precipitated by the election of the anti-Treaty Fianna Fail party led by Eamon de Valera to a majority in the Southern parliament. On taking office, de Valera removed the Oath of Allegiance to the British monarchy from the South's constitution. At the same time, he announced that the South would cease paying land annuities; the money due to the United Kingdom from Irish tenant-purchasers who, prior to the Treaty, had received loans from the British exchequer to buy the land they worked.[5]

The removal of the Oath and the cessation of land annuities brought a harsh reaction from the British. This principally took the form of the imposition of custom duties on imported Irish cattle and other agricultural produce. These measures were opposed by the Labour opposition in parliament, who directed their criticism at J.H. Thomas now responsible for Britain's 'economic war' against the South of Ireland.

When de Valera announced the removal of the Oath, Thomas reacted by accusing him of 'a violation of the Treaty'[6] and of 'breaking the peace'.[7]

Labour members sprang to the defence of the Irish government. David Kirkwood made the point: 'When that contract [Treaty] was made the Irish felt themselves to be a subject race... they now feel they are a free people and are asserting their rights as a free people'.[8]

Thomas also came under Labour fire when he announced the imposition of the customs duties. George Lansbury, leader of the Labour Party, observed: 'When history comes to record what is being done tonight it will be said that a strong and powerful nation, with goodwill on its lips, embarked on an enterprise of trying to coerce and crush a weaker nation into submission'.[9]

Thomas saw no reason to accept such criticism. He who had petitioned Lloyd George to give in to McSweeney now boasted in a private letter: 'I am the first Minister that ever stood up to the Irish, and remember that I am doing it quite determined to maintain British rights and interests'.[10]

The Labour Party's objections to the economic war against the Southern Irish was indicative of a more general attitude, albeit one that was rarely expressed. By and large, all parties in Britain accepted the 1921 assumption that the Irish issue had been settled. When the occasional sign appeared to suggest that this was not the case, then a statement would be made in Parliament. In the Labour Party and elsewhere attention to Ireland did not go beyond that. As early as the 1926 Labour Party conference, Sam Kyle of the Labour Party of Northern Ireland had said of partition that he 'did not think the people who attended the Labour Party conference took any particular interest in this problem'.[11]

Such an apathy was fuelled by a convention that had grown up at Westminster that the internal affairs of Northern Ireland were not for open discussion, a ruling which had little legal basis.[12] When Labour members did ask questions in the Commons on events in the North they were usually harmless. Thus, in the aftermath of the 1935 riots in Belfast, when Unionist supporters attacked Catholic areas and left nine people dead, George Lansbury called on the British Home Secretary to organise a conference of church leaders so as to end 'this terrible sectarian bigotry',[13] although other Labour MPs did call for a full inquiry into the riots.[14]

Organisations like the National Council for Civil Liberties sought to highlight the abuses of Unionist power in the North,[15] but the Labour Party at all levels showed no wish to get involved in campaigning against these abuses. Only when Ireland intruded on British consciousness was there any reaction. At times, Labour responses to the difficulties the 1921 settlement had caused were sympathetic, as the parliamentary opinions expressed on the economic war suggest. On other occasions they were not. In July 1939 the Tory government tabled its Prevention of Violence Bill (Temporary Provisions). This sought to deal with a bombing campaign in Britain, launched by the IRA earlier in the year. Among the Bill's proposals was one giving the Home Secretary the right to deport, without trial, suspected members of the IRA. Although 15 Labour MPs voted against the measure, the official view of the Labour opposition in parliament was to back the Bill in its entirety. It was Labour convert William Benn who explained his party's attitude.

'We are not dividing against the second reading,' he reported, 'because if a Labour government were in power it would maintain public order just as firmly as a Conservative Government'.[16]

Within two months of William Benn giving this assurance, Britain had other bombs to worry about than those placed by the IRA. The second world war began in September 1939 and its course and aftermath once again brought the Labour Party face to face with the Irish question.

Its victory at the 1945 election gave Labour an overall parliamentary majority for the first time in its history, with 393 Labour candidates being returned, 146 more than the other parties combined.

The election was won on a manifesto pledged to, 'the establishment of a Socialist Commonwealth of Great Britain'. During the campaign many Labour candidates had, with some eloquence, told of their visions of the new order that was about to dawn. Thus, Denis Healey, wearing the uniform of a British Army officer, told the Labour Party conference in 1945 that its foreign policy, 'should be to protect, assist, encourage and aid in every way that socialist revolution wherever it appears'.

Referring to the liberation struggles of wartime Europe, Healey concluded:

> The upper classes in every country are selfish, depraved, dissolute and decadent. These upper classes look to the British Army and British people to protect them against the just wrath of the people who have been fighting underground against them for the past four years. We must see that that does not happen.[17]

The views of the young Healey were not shared by everyone in the Labour Party. One dissenter was Herbert Morrison, the Deputy Prime Minister and Lord President of Council. Morrison was to play an important part in the argument over Ireland which lasted the lifetime of the government.

In September 1946 Morrison took advantage of a holiday in Ireland to visit political leaders in the North and South. It was not his first acquaintance with Irish politics. As Home Secretary in the coalition government during the war he had paid regular visits to Northern Ireland, for which the Home Office was then constitutionally responsible. Morrison had been so impressed with what he saw that when he returned from Belfast in July 1943 he addressed the Thirties Club in London at a dinner where Northern Ireland Prime Minister Sir Basil Brooke was guest of honour.

Morrison went out of his way to praise Northern Ireland's loyalty to Britain, lauding it as, 'almost aggressive in nature'. He speculated that the North's participation in the war, in contrast to Southern neutrality, was 'bound to have a permanently modifying effect on many people's opinions' in Great Britain.[18]

After visiting Brooke again in September 1946, Morrison once more sang the praises of the Northern Ireland Premier and his Unionist Party in a memorandum to the Cabinet:

> Sir Basil is always most reasonable and co-operative... the Unionist Party is by no means wholly a Conservative Party. It includes Conservatives, but a large proportion of the members are of a Liberal or Radical tradition; in this country some of them, such as Mr Grant, the Minister of Labour, who is a trade unionist, would almost certainly belong to the Labour Party.[19].

This was an eccentric series of judgements. William Grant was indeed a trade unionist, being a former shipyard worker, but his political views were hardly at one with those traditionally to be found in the British Labour Party. On the foundation of the Northern Ireland state, he had declared that the Unionist Party, 'would not tolerate Sinn Fein and Bolshevism in the six counties'.[20] He was later to boast that the Ulster Special Constabulary, eventually disbanded because of its sectarianism by Labour in 1969, was 'composed entirely of loyal Protestant working men... there are no Roman Catholics among the Special Constabulary'.[21]

Such sentiments were common coinage in the Unionist Party. Morrison's 'reasonable and co-operative' Sir Basil Brooke observed on one occasion:

> Many in the audience employ Catholics, but I have not one about the house... In Northern Ireland the Catholic population is increasing to a great extent. Ninety-seven per cent of Roman Catholics in Ireland are disloyal and disruptive... If we in Ulster allow Roman Catholics to work on our farms we are traitors to Ulster.[22]

It is inconceivable that Herbert Morrison did not have an awareness of the practices of Basil Brooke and his colleagues, so why, in 1946, did Labour's Deputy Prime Minister present himself to his Cabinet colleagues as an apologist for the Orange state? Apart from the strict limitations Morrison placed on his own version of socialism, the chief reason was the part played in the second world war by the loyal subjects in Northern Ireland. Morrison was reported as feeling resentful of the wartime lack of patriotism to Britain of not just the Irish Republic, but of Northern Irish Catholics as well.[23]

The future of Northern Ireland was a topic of discussion at the other important political encounter Morrison had in September 1946. This was with Eamon de Valera, who had been in power for 14 years. Given the history of opposition to partition by the Labour Party, de Valera may have felt, now that Labour was in power in Britain, that it was opportune to raise again the question of the division of his country. When he did broach the subject with Morrison on 12 September, he was given little encouragement. Morrison recorded his own attitude in the same Cabinet memorandum which had praised the Unionists:

> My own personal feeling was that the wisest course on all sides was not to hurry the partition issue. Time was a great healer and I hoped it would be a great healer between the three parties concerned, namely Great Britain, Eire and Northern Ireland, but if the issue was raised in any precipitate manner, first class trouble might ensue. From the fairly close knowledge of Northern Ireland I had gained as Home Secretary, I was quite sure that Northern Ireland would not be a consenting party, at any rate in anything like the early future. On the contrary, they would be very actively hostile. They had deep feelings about their rights and allegiances...
>
> Moreover, the war had not improved the situation... Eire had remained neutral in the war. As a purely practical matter, British public opinion noted that the Northern Ireland ports and airfields were of greatest value to our war effort.
>
> This was altogether apart from the great loyalty of the British people and of Ulster to the Crown...
>
> All this was to say nothing of the potential dynamite involved in religious differences between North and South.
>
> In all circumstances, I personally thought, that from every point of view much was to be gained and nothing was to be lost by a policy of developing good co-operative relations... but not precipitating the issue of partition... there was plenty of trouble in the world already.[24]

Morrison in his talks with de Valera had been given no specific mandate from the Labour Cabinet. The meeting was an informal one, arranged because Morrison happened to be holidaying in Ireland. Nevertheless, in being so forthright, Morrison must have been confident that the attitude he outlined to de Valera would get the backing of the rest of the Cabinet.

When he circulated his memorandum, the first member of the government to respond was Viscount Addison. As Secretary of State for Dominion Affairs, he was responsible for Britain's relations with Eire and, like Morrison, was on the right wing of the Party. He endorsed Morrison's memorandum in a note to the Cabinet on 18 October.

> To my mind, there are two essential considerations. First, the attitude of the majority of the inhabitants of the six counties of Northern Ireland. It is clear they are determined to oppose any form of union with Eire... Religion, loyalty to the Crown and the British connection, and material interests are all factors which govern their attitude...
>
> But in our own interests also it seems to me that on strategic grounds we must bear in mind the lessons of the last war. The retention of a base in Northern Ireland for the protection of shipping was one of the principle factors which enabled us to carry on... In the light of this it would be folly on our part to throw away the safeguard of our security provided by our present position in Northern Ireland...
>
> I have no desire that we on this side should discourage the North and South of Ireland in any move that they may make with the object of getting together. As a long term policy it is no doubt right and indeed inevitable that Northern Ireland and Eire should enter into some kind of closer relationship. But as the Lord President said it is for Eire to give as well as take. I am sure therefore that for the present our only safe course is to maintain silence...
>
> Generally, I am sure that we ought to continue the policy which I and my predecessors in the Dominions Office have followed, and decline to be drawn on the matter of partition.[25]

This was the return to the familiar theme which had occupied Labour Party leaders 25 years before: that Irish self-determination was conditional on a guarantee that an independent Ireland would not be a military or naval menace to Great Britain. Yet Addison and Morrison had gone further. British strategic interest now ruled out, except in a meaningless 'long term' sense, the possibility of Ireland ever attaining unity and freedom of action. This was all the more disingenuous since Morrison's memorandum had admitted that de Valera would be sympathetic towards a defence treaty with Britain in the event of a united Ireland.[26]

Morrison's memorandum and Addison's comments were

discussed at a full meeting of the Cabinet on 29 October. The minutes record that the ministers 'took note, with approval' the advice offered by Morrison and Addison.[27]

To the 1945-51 Labour government's chagrin, events in Ireland itself continued to display their ability to upset the best laid plans of British politicians. Almost two years to the day after Morrison's meeting with de Valera, John A. Costello, the newly elected Irish Taoiseach (Premier) visited Ottawa and told Canada and the world of his government's intention to take the South of Ireland out of the Commonwealth, and to declare the state a Republic.

In a Cabinet discussion on 28 October 1948 Labour Prime Minister Clement Attlee assessed what might be the motivation of these moves:

> Behind the immediate issue lay the [Irish] government's determination to end partition and there was little doubt that they recognised that they would be in a better position to put pressure on the United Kingdom government once Eire had become a foreign country...
>
> No further obstacle would be placed in the way of Eire's admission to the United Nations and it would be open to her to raise the question of partition in the General Assembly.[28]

Although Costello's decision to take the South out of the Commonwealth did herald a new attack on partition, that was not all that was involved. The declaration of the Republic was only the latest stage in 16 years of dismantling the Treaty of 1921.

But the sympathy shown by Labour in the early thirties towards the South of Ireland's efforts to determine its own policies were not apparent in the reactions of the Labour government in 1948-49. In that first major discussion in the Cabinet on 28 October 1948 the warning that Addison had given in 1946 was echoed. The discussion concluded:

> The United Kingdom government has hitherto maintained the attitude that partition was an issue for settlement by the Irish themselves. But Eire's secession from the Commonwealth would raise acutely the issue whether, for defence reasons, it was possible any longer to maintain that attitude... It was likely that the government of Northern Ireland would feel bound to adopt rigorous measures in the protection of her interests.[29]

The initial response of government ministers was to punish the South severely for declaring a Republic and leaving the Commonwealth, decisions which were embodied in the repeal of the South's External Relations Act. The Irish were most vulnerable with regard to citizenship and trade, and the British Labour government did consider taking retaliatory action in these areas, and treating the South, henceforth, as an entirely foreign country. This was discussed at a series of meetings in Paris on the 14, 15 and 16 November between British ministers, representatives of the Southern government and the Prime Ministers of New Zealand, Australia and Canada. The latter were in Europe for the Commonwealth Conference. A British Cabinet memorandum, drawn up by Herbert Morrison and Philip Noel-Baker, Secretary of State for Commonwealth Relations, reported the outcome of these meetings:

> It thus became clear to us that, if we persisted in the view that Eire must be regarded as a foreign country once the External Relations Act was repealed, we should find ourselves alone in maintaining this view. It was plain that Canada, Australia and New Zealand, like Eire, wished to follow the contrary view: and they all felt so strongly on this point that it seemed likely that they might press it to the point of public disagreement with the United Kingdom government. This would have been so serious a development that we thought it right... to explore the possibility of divising legal means of supporting the argument that Eire and Commonwealth countries would not become foreign to one another.[30]

The Southern Irish had been saved from vindictive treatment by the intervention of other Commonwealth leaders. The Prime Ministers of Canada, New Zealand and Australia felt no compulsion to upset existing relations between their country and the South of Ireland for the sake of mere vengeance.

The Eire government had, on occasions, sought to play down the importance of the whole affair. Sean MacBride, Minister for External Relations, in an interview with the *Manchester Guardian* suggested:

> As a constitutional fiction the External Relations Act pleased no one and when it goes the British government will realise that such worn out constitutional fictions are only reminders of a not too happy past and form a barrier to better relationships.[31]

Even Attlee was later to admit to the House of Commons that treating Southern Irish citizens as foreigners would have presented immense practical problems:

> As everybody knows, there are in Britain large numbers of people of Irish descent, some born in Eire and some born in this country, and there is a continual passage to and fro of people who come over to work or to study or for pleasure. It would be an extremely difficult thing to decide in every case from day to day as to what the exact status was of a person with an Irish name, and if we had had to make all citizens of Eire aliens, it would have involved a great expenditure of men and money and great extension of the control of aliens. We had in particular also to remember the difficulties caused because of the fact of the land frontier between Northern Ireland, which is part of the United Kingdom and the Commonwealth, and Eire.[32]

In the light of subsequent claims by Labour spokespersons that the British government treated Eire generously in regards to the action taken over the repeal of the External Relations Act,[23] it is important to stress what Attlee was conceding in his statement: that the decision not to treat the South as a foreign country was not taken benevolently, but for practical considerations. It has only become apparent with the release of Cabinet papers that it was the restraining hands of other Commonwealth countries which tempered the Labour government's sense of British outrage.

Their wrath found other outlets. On 28 October 1948 Attlee told the House of Commons: 'The view of His Majesty's Government of the United Kingdom has always been that no change should be made in the constitutional status of Northern Ireland without Northern Ireland's free agreement'.[34]

Attlee's use of the word 'always' is interesting. Whether he was referring to his government or to all previous Majesty's governments since 1921 is unclear, but in considering the stance on partition which Attlee and his colleagues were to elaborate, it is worth establishing what exactly was the constitutional position on the partition of Ireland.

The 1920 Government of Ireland Act had envisaged that the division of Ireland would be temporary. The 'Summary of Main Provisions' of that Act stated:

Although at the beginning there are to be two parliaments
and two governments of Ireland, the Act contemplates and
affords every facility for union between North and South,
and empowers the two parliaments by mutual agreement and
joint action to terminate partition and to set up one parliament and one government for the whole of Ireland. With a
view to the eventual establishment of a single parliament, and
to bringing about harmonious action between the two
parliaments and governments, there is created a bound of
union in the meantime by means of a Council of Ireland
which is to consist of twenty representatives elected by each
parliament and a president nominated by the Lord Lieutenant.
It will fall to members of the body to initiate proposals for
united action on the part of the two parliaments and to bring
forward these proposals in the respective parliaments.[35]

Although this Act was to undergo some amendments as a
consequence of the Anglo-Irish Treaty, the body of the legislation quoted above remained in force.

The Council never met, but that did not alter the fact that
the division of Ireland was not envisaged as being permanent.

By stating that the 'free agreement' of Northern Ireland
would be necessary for any change in that state's constitutional
status, Attlee was not only disavowing the hopes for unity built
into the Treaty, he was for the first time introducing the principle
of the right of Northern Ireland to veto any alteration in their
border.

A veto had been invented, but what was envisaged in practice? Basil Brooke and the Unionist set about removing any
ambiguity. The Northern Ireland Prime Minister took advantage of an invitation to stay with Attlee at Chequers on 28
November to press his views. Attlee reported to the Cabinet:

Sir Basil Brooke said that his immediate anxieties would be
allayed if he could be given an assurance that the constitutional position of Northern Ireland would not be prejudiced by
Eire ceasing to be a member of the Commonwealth. I gave
him, on behalf of the United Kingdom government, an
assurance that the constitutional position of Northern Ireland
would be safeguarded, and I added, in reply to a further question, that he was at liberty to say publicly that he had received
that assurance.[36]

Brooke had told Attlee that he would report their conversa-
tion to Unionist MPs in both the Northern Ireland and United

Kingdom parliaments. He hinted that there might still be trouble ahead by adding that he 'hoped this might have some influence in restraining these members from raising unnecessary difficulties'.[37]

The nature of the 'safeguards' promised by Attlee were still to be resolved. At a Cabinet meeting on 22 November a working party of high-level civil servants, headed by the Secretary to the Cabinet, Norman Brook, had been established to look into this area. Their report explains the subsequent actions of the Labour government.

It brought together the various strands of opinion that had been expressed by different Labour ministers on Northern Ireland from Morrison's memorandum of 1946 onwards. It also offered conclusions:

> The government of Northern Ireland has asked that statutory force should now be given to the assurance which the Prime Minister gave on 28 October... that 'no change shall be made in the constitutional status of Northern Ireland without Northern Ireland's free agreement'... it has been ascertained that the government of Northern Ireland... would probably be content if statutory force could be given to the simple assurance... that Northern Ireland should not cease to be part of the United Kingdom without the consent of the Northern Ireland parliament.
>
> Now that Eire will shortly cease to owe any allegiance to the Crown, it has become a matter of first class strategic importance to this country that the North should continue to form part of His Majesty's dominions. So far as can be foreseen, it will never be to Great Britain's advantage that Northern Ireland should form part of a territory outside His Majesty's jurisdiction. Indeed it seems unlikely that Great Britain would ever be able to agree to this even if the people of Northern Ireland desired it.[38]

There were two innovative features in Brook's report, the general lines of which were accepted at a Cabinet meeting in early January 1949. First, the suggestion that it would be the will of the Northern Ireland parliament which would be the determining factor in any possible constitutional change in Northern Ireland's status. Second, and in obvious contradiction to the first, the suggestion that whatever the population of Northern Ireland 'desired' Britain would hold on to the North.

The first point became clause 1(1)B of the 1949 Ireland Act:

Parliament hereby declares that Northern Ireland remains
part of His Majesty's Dominions and of the United Kingdom
and affirms that in no event will Northern Ireland or any part
thereof cease to be part of His Majesty's Dominions and of
the United Kingdom without the consent of the Parliament of
Northern Ireland.

The South of Ireland's repeal of the External Relations Act did
require the passing of reciprocal legislation at Westminster, but
there was nothing in the wording of that repeal which made it in-
cumbent on Britain to even refer to the partition of Ireland or
to the constitutional status of the North in its parallel legislation.

The Attlee government's decision to write it in was political,
motivated by the Cabinet's overall approach to Northern
Ireland since the Morrison memorandum of September 1946.
They would avoid, if possible, any reference to partition, but, if
pressed, would come out in support of it. When pressure came,
it was not so much from the South, but from the Unionists in
Northern Ireland. The Brook report makes clear it was, initially,
the Northern Ireland government which 'asked that statutory
force should now be given' to the right of Northern Ireland to
veto any constitutional alterations. The same point is found in
the minutes of a meeting between British government ministers
and leaders of the Northern Ireland government in early
January 1949. Attlee told the Unionists:

The United Kingdom were most anxious to help the government of Northern Ireland. The United Kingdom government
had, in particular, considered the request of the government
of Northern Ireland that legislation should be enacted by
Parliament at Westminster to safeguard the constitutional
position of Northern Ireland. Mr Attlee suggested that a
preferable course would be to include in the body of the Bill
[Ireland Act]... an affirmation by parliament that in no event
would Northern Ireland cease to be part of the United
Kingdom except with the consent of the Parliament of Northern Ireland.[37]

Not surprisingly, the minutes of this meeting record that
Basil Brooke 'welcomed an affirmation on these lines'.

The extent of the Labour government's capitulation to the
Unionists is further illustrated by another issue which arose

from the discussions on the Ireland Act. Point 26 of Norman Brook's working party report recorded that: 'The government of Northern Ireland ask that there should be a six months' residence qualification for the Westminster elections'.

The motivation for the request was explained by Attlee in his report of the meeting between British and Northern Ireland ministers:

> The Northern Ireland Ministers pressed strongly their suggestion that there should be a six month residence qualification for the exercise in Northern Ireland of the Westminster franchise. They feel very strongly that they are entitled to ask for protection against the danger that Eire citizens will get their names on the register by paying short visits to Northern Ireland around the qualifying date... they are genuinely apprehensive that this may be one of the strategems employed in furtherance of the anti-partition campaign which the Eire government are fostering.[40]

Apparently Clement Attlee shared the Unionist' rather paranoiac apprehensions. His report to the Cabinet concluded: 'There is undoubtedly some risk in this respect and it is difficult to deny Northern Ireland the protection for which it asks'.

The Cabinet was not in complete agreement with Attlee and eventually the residence qualification was whittled down to three months. In return for this additional concession to the Unionists, the Labour Cabinet decided to press for a lowering of the residence qualification for voting in the Northern Ireland parliamentary elections. This stood at a massive seven years.

The Attlee Cabinet resolved to press Basil Brooke to lower the residential qualifications. The challenge was not particularly formidable... the request was that the seven years be cut to five. But even that was too much for the confident Unionists. Attlee explained to his colleagues:

> On 12 January the Cabinet asked me to make a further attempt to persuade the Prime Minister of Northern Ireland to reduce the residential qualifications for the franchise for the Northern Ireland parliament in return for the introduction of a residential qualification of three months for the exercise in Northern Ireland of Westminster franchise.
>
> I have had a further discussion with Sir Basil Brooke on this point. He has assured me that his government gave the most careful consideration to this proposal, and would have

been glad if they could have helped the Home Secretary to meet the criticisms which are likely to be raised at Westminster by any proposal to amend the law in relation to elections in Northern Ireland. They were satisfied that it would be politically impossible to put this proposal before their parliament at the present time.[41]

Again Attlee acquiesced, saying, 'I find it difficult to resist these arguments'.[42]

The one area where the Labour Cabinet found it possible to resist the demands of the Unionists was in the field of semantics. Basil Brooke had requested that the title of the Northern Ireland state be changed to 'Ulster', to eliminate any suggestion that the six counties were, in any way, 'Irish'. Brooke also requested that the Westminster government refrain from referring to the South as 'the Republic of Ireland', because, he said, this implied acceptance of the claim in the 1938 constitution of Southern Ireland to all 32 counties in Ireland. Attlee and his colleagues were unable to agree to these suggestions. On 'Ulster', it was pointed out, the geographical description of the term meant nine counties. On 'the Republic of Ireland', Attlee explained the diplomatic difficulties involved in naming a state anything other than that which the state called itself.

Basil Brooke remained dissatisfied and, in the discussion with Attlee and Home Secretary Chuter Ede on 18 January, he made a remarkable threat. The minutes of the meeting record that Brooke warned:

> He might be pressed to put forward the demand that Northern Ireland should be given dominion status, so that the Northern Ireland parliament might have full powers to do all that it thought necessary for the protection of the North. This, he thought, would be an unsound solution of Ulster difficulties and he did not wish to be put into a position in which he would have to advocate it.[43]

Considering that the union with Britain was the founding principle of Basil Brooke's political party, this statement appears so extraordinary that it requires a brief explanation. It was not the first time, or the last, in the history of Unionism that its political leaders had threatened secession from the United Kingdom. During the Home Rule controversy of 1912-21, Edward Carson frequently threatened a unilateral declaration of dependence (UDI) from Britain by Ulster, once going as far as to threaten to seek an alliance with the German Kaiser.[44] During the 1970s, another leading Unionist, William Craig, was also to allude to UDI, and at the end of the 1970s the paramilitary Ulster Defence Association would lend its support to the idea of an independent 'Ulster'.

For many Unionists the union with Britain has never been anything other than a means to an end: loyalist control of as much as Ireland as possible. If the link with Britain itself ever jeopardised that control, it was dispensable.

However, it is unlikely that the Brooke Unionists gave in 1949 any serious contemplation to quitting the United Kingdom. At any rate, on that occasion the Unionist bluff was called and the 'Republic of Ireland' entered the language of British diplomacy.

When Brooke made his threat on 18 January, he was probably more concerned with firing a warning shot against any backtracking by the British on the promises already given to his Unionists. As early as November 1948 Brooke had raised the spectre of the Protestant backlash with his reference to the difficulties in 'restraining' his supporters. There is also the evidence of a Cabinet meeting of 12 January 1949 at which Attlee and his colleagues argued in favour of clause 1(1)B of the Ireland Act on the grounds that it would head off 'a revival of the Ulster Volunteers'.[45]

It would, nevertheless, be a misjudgement to conclude that in conceding to the Unionists most of their demands, the postwar Labour government was primarily deferring to Unionist blackmail. Rather, the 1949 Ireland Act represented a convergence of like minds. The Northern Ireland Unionists, the British civil service headed by Norman Brook and the Labour Cabinet were one in the view that the partition of Ireland needed to be made more permanent.

For the British, the central motivation was located in the field of defence, and in that there is continuity with the preoccupations of the Labour leaders of thirty years before. In 1918-20, however, those leaders did not go unchallenged in their efforts to contain the boundaries of Irish freedom. What remains to be explored is whether a similar fight was waged in 1949.

6. 'Against Every Decent Principle'

A month before the Ireland Bill was presented to parliament, the Labour Party produced a policy statement, which was to be the basis of its manifesto for the 1950 general election. By socialist standards, 'Labour Believes in Britain' was unambitious. It was a step backwards from the reforming zeal of the previous three years and committed Labour to the principle of the mixed economy. Such general moderation did not augur well for a challenge by the rank and file on government policy on Ireland.

By 1949, the complexities surrounding the Irish question must have been little more than a faint memory for most Labour Party members. Yet the government's cementing of partition did not go unquestioned.

The first challenge came from the Minister of Civil Aviation Lord Pakenham (later Lord Longford). Though not a member of the Cabinet, his special knowledge of Irish affairs secured his attendance at a crucial meeting on 12 January 1949 when the final, major decisions on the Ireland Bill were to be taken.

Amongst the items to be discussed was a letter from Pakenham:

> Prime Minister,
> Thank you for allowing me to come to the Cabinet tomorrow when Ireland is under discussion. As you know I am Irish on my father's side, and have kept in touch with Irish politics for a good many years. I also published in 1935 what is still the standard work on the Anglo-Irish Treaty of 1921,[1] incidently dealing at some length with the peculiar origin of the present boundary between North and South Ireland.
>
> At the Cabinet tomorrow, I should hope to make briefly but emphatically the following points:
> (i) No decision taken now should be allowed to prejudge the question whether the unification of Ireland is or is not

desirable from the British standpoint.

(ii) The one satisfactory solution of the Anglo-Irish problem is the political unity of Ireland, coupled with the strategic unity of the two islands. In other words, the end of partition and a close defensive arrangement, no doubt as part of Western union or the Atlantic Pact between Britain and *the whole of Ireland*.

(iii) Any explicit guarantee of the territorial integrity of Northern Ireland would be, in my opinion, absolutely wrong. The present frontier, which includes in the North two dissident counties out of a total of six, is quite indefensible.

(iv) The record of the Northern Irish government since Northern Ireland was established in 1920 has revealed an attitude to freedom of speech, [to] a fair delimitation of constituency boundaries and to democracy generally which is quite out of keeping with our Labour ideas, and for that matter those of other British parties, except the Communists. Any efforts on their part to obtain greater powers to deal with their own electoral arrangements should be studied with greatest caution.

Pakenham.[2]

Pakenham's letter was primarily a restatement of the arguments advanced by Labour Party leaders in 1920, in short, the advocacy of a united Ireland, tied defensively to Britain. His innovation was the reference to the political situation within Northern Ireland since partition.

The Secretary to the Cabinet, Norman Brook, who along with Herbert Morrison had become the chief proponents of Unionism during the discussions on the Bill, briefed Clement Attlee on Pakenham's visit to the Cabinet:

Lord Pakenham... represents only one side of this controversy and there are large sections of opinion in this country which will expect the government to take a firm line in support of the North. Much of this Bill consists of provisions which can be represented as 'concessions' to the South; and I should have thought that, politically, it was important that these should be balanced by some provisions designed to give support to the North.[3]

Brook's view proved persuasive. The Cabinet meeting on 12 January was, for Pakenham, unproductive. The minutes recorded:

The Minister of Civil Aviation said that he thought it would be a mistake to give any guarantee of the territorial integrity of Northern Ireland. In two Northern counties there was a majority in favour of ending partition and, if the issue of partition ever came before an international court, the view might be expressed that these counties should be transferred to Eire. He believed that the right solution lay in the strategic unity of Ireland and the United Kingdom.

The general feeling of the Cabinet was, however, in favour of a statutory declaration [clause 1(1)B]... It was by no means certain that an international tribunal, if the issue were brought before it, would consider that the two counties of Tyrone and Fermanagh should be transferred to Eire... Unless the people of Northern Ireland felt reasonably assured of the support of the people of this country there might be a revival of the Ulster Volunteers and of other bodies intending to meet any threat of force by force; and this would bring nearer the danger of an outbreak of violence in Ireland. From the point of view of Great Britain experience in the last war has amply proved that Northern Ireland's continued adhesion to the United Kingdom was essential for her defence. In 1940 Eire had jeopardised her chances of ending partition by remaining neutral.[4]

The reference to the neutrality of the South during the second world war requires a brief explanation. In 1938, under the Anglo-Irish agreements, the British government headed by Neville Chamberlain had agreed to evacuate the Eire naval bases Britain had retained in the 1921 Treaty. These Agreements effectively recognised the right of the South to exercise an independent foreign policy, despite Eire's membership of the Commonwealth.

The outbreak of the second world war saw the South adopt a policy of neutrality. As early as 1936, de Valera had precipitated the stance:

All the small states can do if the statesmen of the greater states fail in their duty is resolutely to determine that they will not become the tools of any great power, and that they will resist with whatever strength they may possess every attempt to force them into a war against their will.[5]

De Valera had also made clear on many occasions that there was no possibility of the South siding with Britain in a war while partition existed. In 1940, Winston Churchill met de Valera secretly and told him that the end of the war would see Britain supporting Irish unity if the South meantime allowed British naval facilities. De Valera, perhaps recalling past British promises, rejected the offer as too vague to sacrifice the neutrality of Ireland.

Yet Irish neutrality was 'friendly' to Britain.[6] Some 50,000 citizens of the South volunteered to serve in the British forces.[7] Northern Ireland's contribution was, of course, more substantial, although, unlike in the rest of the UK, conscription did not apply.

What does not appear in the minutes of that Cabinet meeting of 12 January 1949, was any response to Pakenham's allegations of political malpractices by the Northern government.

Embarrassingly for the Labour Cabinet, and crucial to the debate in parliament which was to follow, fresh evidence supporting Pakenham's criticisms of Unionist rule was supplied when Basil Brooke called a snap Northern Ireland general election for 10 February. According to the Unionist manifesto, the issue was clear:

> Our country is in danger... today we fight to defend our every existence and the heritage of our Ulster children. The British government have agreed to abide by the decision of the Ulster people. It is therefore imperative that our determination to remain under the Union Jack should be immediately and overwhelmingly re-affirmed... 'No surrender, We are King's men'.[8]

Throughout the history of the Northern Ireland state the Unionists had sought to make every election a referendum on the union — which was one way of avoiding examination of their vulnerable social and economic policies. But in February 1949 there was justification for centring the election on the issue of partition. The South's repeal of the External Relations Act, the British government's insertion of partition into the Ireland Bill and the formation in the South of an all-party campaign opposed to partition inevitably meant the issue of Irish unity became dominant in the electoral period.

Even by the Northern Ireland standards the election was a squalid affair. The electoral registers were years out of date and favoured the Unionist candidates. Many non-Unionists had their meetings attacked and broken up. In one incident on 1 February, the anti-partition Labour candidate Jack Beattie was stoned by several thousand Unionists during an East Belfast meeting. A leading Unionist, Lord Glentoran, explained the attacked as a consequence of 'excitement in Ballymaracarrett where Mr Beattie was born and bred and where he has now turned his back on his own people and his own king'.[9] Basil Brooke ended his campaign by inviting voters: 'to cross the Boyne... with me as your leader and to fight for the same cause as King William fought for in days gone by'.[10] Even Attlee muttered at Westminster that elections in Northern Ireland, 'are not conducted on quite the same lines as we have over here'.[11] As many as 200 Labour MPs went further, demanding the postponement of the election until it could be staged in free and democratic conditions. The motion was never discussed.

The Ireland Bill was finally debated in the Commons in May 1949. The second reading was introduced by Attlee who attempted to present the Bill as uncontentious. On the Bill's conferring to the North the right to veto on any future constitutional change, the Prime Minister declared: 'I cannot understand why the Clause should seem to evoke a great deal of opposition and heated protest. I am bound to say that I think these protests are based on a misapprehension'.[12] Attlee's main tactic in deflecting criticism of clause 1(1)B was to blame the Southern government:

> I think it is obvious to anybody who thought on these subjects that the action of the government of Eire in deciding to leave the Commonwealth would increase the difficulty of arriving at any agreement on the partition question...
>
> I do not intend to deal at any length this afternoon with the partition question. That would be harking back to the old unhappy days, days before all of us but a mere handful were in this House. We have to deal with the position as it exists. However, the government of Eire decided to proceed with taking these steps to leave the Commonwealth, and I pointed out to them that this would inevitably make more difficulties in arriving at their other objective, the unification of Ireland.[13]

Attlee's remarks were endorsed by Tory opposition speakers. This first public airing of the bipartisan approach to Irish politics which was to become so familiar two decades later was noted by one of the first Labour critics to take part in the debate, Hugh Delargy:

We saw today a remarkable degree of agreement between the Prime Minister and the Right Hon. Member for Warwick and Leamington [Anthony Eden, Conservative Deputy-Leader]. When the Right Hon. Gentleman gives us his Unionist and Conservative views I listen to them with attention and, indeed, with respect, because I know he sincerely holds these views, but when my own leader, the Prime Minister, addresses me in the same accents I listen indeed with attention but also with acute alarm.[14]

Delargy went on to launch a wide-ranging attack on clause 1(1)B, describing it as 'irrelevant' to the main purpose of the Bill' because it ensures that 'partition becomes permanent', and saying, that the government was proposing to, 'take sides for the first time in the quarrel about Irish unity. They take the Tory and the Unionist side, against the democratic Labour and Nationalist side'.

Delargy then posed three questions. He wanted to know whether the government, in light of the new authority being handed to the Northern Ireland parliament, was prepared to support any measures to protect the minority who came under the jurisdiction of that parliament. The answer — as will be illustrated shortly — was no. Delargy went on to demand: 'Who insisted on the inclusion of this unnecessary, irrelevant and quite mischievous clause?' The reply he did not receive would have been 'the Unionist Government in Northern Ireland', although the Labour government in Westminster needed little persuasion. Delargy then asked whether other members of the Commonwealth had been consulted about the partition clause. Again he got no answer and there is no evidence in any Cabinet papers of such consultation.

Delargy ended with an appeal to the government's socialist conscience:

The Irish people have the moral right to decide for themselves their own destiny. The territorial integrity of Ireland is a matter to be determined democratically by the free vote of the Irish people and by no one else. This clause denies them that right...

I appeal to the government to withdraw this clause. I appeal to the government as one of their most consistent and loyal supporters to withdraw it because it is not only bad in itself: it goes against every decent principle for which the

Labour Party ever stood. I would remind my own leaders on the Front Bench that when the 1920 Act was passed in this House, which first divided Ireland in two, the Parliamentary Labour Party of those days unanimously, officially and enthusiastically voted against it...

Therefore not only in support of the clear democratic rights of the Irish people, but also for the good name of this country and for the good name of the party to which I belong, I would urge the government to reconsider the whole matter, to seek a fresh basis from which this very difficult problem could be approached. If the government were to do that they would have with them not merely the friendly co-operation of the Irish people in Ireland and in many countries of the world, but they would also have the heartiest goodwill of democrats everywhere.[15]

Two anti-partition Northern Irish MPs moved and seconded an amendment to delete the controversial clause. One was Jack Beattie, a former Protestant shipyard worker and ex-member of the Independent Labour Party who had been elected for West Belfast as an anti-partition Labour candidate. The other was Anthony Mulvey, first elected for Fermanagh and South Tyrone in 1935, but who had refused to attend the Commons until 1945. Ironically, Mulvey and his supporters had abandoned abstentionism because they believed a Labour government would be friendly to Irish aspirations.[16]

Neither Beattie nor Mulvey could hide their feelings of bitterness or betrayal. 'When constitutional reform is refused, the physical force movement emerges,' warned Beattie,[17] and, even more prophetically, 'so long as partition remains, so long will British governments find it haunting them'.[18]

Mulvey's plea to Labour back-benchers to vote against their government stressed what he saw as the particularly perfidy of the Labour leaders — that previously 'a Labour administration at Westminster was always looked on by Irish people as friends of Ireland', but now 'no government who have been in office for a long time have done more to perpetuate partition than the present Labour government'.[19]

Herbert Morrison summed up for the government at the conclusion of the second reading. He was not the most sensitive of choices but at least, unlike Attlee, he made no attempt to hide the government's motives in proposing clause 1(1)B. Morrison began with a geographical observation that Ireland, 'is very close to our shores and we cannot be indifferent to the circumstances which obtain there'. He spoke of the good luck that country had experienced in being closely located to Britain. Referring to the South's decision to leave the Commonwealth, he declared: 'I think it is the case that if Ireland had been situated close to some other great powers and countries in the world, the change would not have come as smoothly as it has done, and that is very fortunate for Ireland'.[20]

He wound up in grand imperial style:

> I do not think anybody in this House would be [for] taking the initiative in urging Northern Ireland to leave the United Kingdom and therefore the Commonwealth. That would be an unthinkable course which would not be approved of by any British electorate... If Irishmen get together and make agreement among themselves that is a situation we will consider, but it is no business of this government — and it is not going to be — to diminish the territory of the United Kingdom.[21]

Thirteen MPs voted against the second reading of the Ireland Bill. They included three anti-partitionists from Northern Ireland, the two Communist MPs and eight Labour members. It was not a substantial revolt, but there were a large number of absentees despite the government imposing a three-line whip.[22] The Bill, together with the defeated amendments deleting clause 1(1)B, went on to committee stage. Just before it was debated there, an external voice of protest was raised. A message from the executive of the Irish Trades Union Congress urged the British TUC general council to call on all Labour MPs to oppose the Bill which raised 'another formidable barrier against the ultimate unity of Ireland'.[23]. The TUC declined to offer any such advice. The leadership of the British labour movement had supported the views of Irish labour in 1920-21, but it opted to ignore them a generation later. The strength of feeling in the South of Ireland was illustrated when a reported 100,000 people demonstrated in Dublin against the partition clause just before the Bill went to the Commons Committee in London.[24]

There were two amendments to clause 1(1)B before the Committee. Jack Beattie's had been introduced at the second reading; the other attempted to wrest the decision on any future constitutional change from the Northern Ireland parliament and place it in the hands of 'the people of Northern Ireland'. The latter was a bid to highlight the undemocratic election practices which secured seats in the North's parliament. Considerable support for both amendments came from the Labour left and from members of the 'Friends of Ireland', an MPs' pressure group established in 1946 and led by Ulster Protestant and Labour left-winger Geoffrey Bing. Jack Beattie, another Ulster Protestant, made clear his feelings: 'Am I to see the day when a political party which I have supported for the whole of my life and which is now in government, is to destroy every reasonable opportunity of bringing into being a united and undivided Ireland?'[25]

Home Secretary Chuter Ede replied for the government. Although not an inspired contribution, it is noteworthy as the only public detailed defence of clause 1(1)B made by the government. He began with an admission:

> I have not a drop of blood other than English in my veins... therefore intervention in an Irish debate is always a matter of some risk, and certainly makes it very difficult to understand the temper of some of the participants in the discussions. ...We are faced today with a completely new situation which is not of our creation. This paragraph... says in the first place that in this matter of the ultimate destiny of North Ireland we are determined that physical force is not to be the arbitrating consideration.[26]

Ede's reference to physical force was prompted by an earlier contribution to the debate from Unionist MP Sir Charles Haughton, who had seen posters in Dublin urging people to arm for an attack on the North. He apparently regarded these examples of Republican rhetoric as serious recruiting calls. Even if they had been, it was a bit late in the political history of Anglo-Irish relations for a British government spokesperson to decry the use of force.

The most interesting part of Ede's speech was his reply to critics of clause 1(1)B. He referred to previous policies of the Labour Party:

> I speak as one who, in 1906 and twice in 1910, voted for Home Rule as an elector, but I voted for Home Rule within the British Commonwealth of Nations... Whether we like it

or not, the majority of the people of Northern Ireland as at present constituted, desire to remain not merely inside the United Kingdom, but inside the British Commonwealth of Nations, and a new situation has been created whereby if Irish unity is to be attained on the basis of the demand of the South, it must now be at the price of going out of the United Kingdom and out of the British Commonwealth of Nations.[27].

In one sense, Ede's argument was a red herring. Had the controversy been confined to the right of Northern Ireland to stay in the Commonwealth, clause 1(1)B could have been limited to that issue. Yet there was some substance in Ede's insistence that the Irish Home Rule and unity which both he and the Labour Party had supported in the opening decades of the century was a limited form of independence. As has been illustrated, the December 1920 conference of the Labour Party had been quite specific in this regard, as was Labour support in parliament for the Anglo-Irish Treaty.

In another sense too, Ede in 1949 was reminiscent of earlier Labour parliamentary spokesmen in his wish that the Irish question would once and for all stop interfering in British politics. Towards the end of his speech he remarked:

I only wish that Irishmen on both sides of the border could some time live for about a fortnight in today, instead of always living in the remote past. I do not think that any Irishman can ever read a history book with great pleasure after he is 20 years of age, for he finds nothing new; he has never forgotten anything.[28]

Ede's arrongance did not win him any new friends among his Labour critics. When the vote was taken 54 MPs voted for one or both the amendments, although only 23, including tellers, supported the more forthright Beattie proposal to delete the partition clause. Nevertheless, the Communist Party's *Daily Worker* heralded the votes as 'two of the biggest revolts in the lifetime of the present parliament'.[29] A few days later, in the same newspaper, Communist MP Willie Gallagher declared of the Ireland Act: 'Surely, never was there such a betrayal'.[30]

Labour's newspaper, the *Daily Herald*, adopted a rather different approach. The day after the third reading of the Bill it drummed up a piece of black propaganda typical of British media coverage of Ireland 20 years later. The front page splashed:

'IRA drills border force', with a sub-headline alleging a plan to 'Seize the six: prepare for action', presumably a reference to the same poster mentioned by the Unionist Sir Charles Haughton two days before. The *Herald* suggested the IRA was poised to launch a mass invasion of the North in association with 'an Irish Society which has fascist ideas'.[31]

The third reading of the Bill was passed with undue haste and little consideration — its parliamentary lifespan from first to third reading took just over a week. Neil Maclean, MP for Glasgow Govan, one-time secretary of the revolutionary Socialist Labour Party and one of three MPs who had been around when partition was imposed, contrasted Labour behaviour over three decades:

> The one thing that strikes me while this Bill is going through the House, is that the Labour government, formed out of the Labour Party, should be taking an entirely different attitude towards Ireland now from that which was taken by the Labour Party in the House of Commons in 1918. That is what vexes me...
>
> In those days the Labour Party were not a government but an opposition of between 40 and 50 hon. members, and they did their best to try and bring satisfaction and peace between the two parties in Ireland...
>
> I voted against the Bill when it first came before the House. I will vote against it tonight if the House is divided. The feelings that I had in those days 30 years ago, with regards to the Irish question are still with me.[32]

If that was the conscience of the Labour left given voice by one of its oldest members, some of the younger MPs felt no such pangs. Michael Foot, rising star of the left, defended his support for the government in the *Daily Herald*. In the first of two articles he protested that the Bill 'does not mean approval of the monstrously undemocratic methods employed by the Northern Ireland government'.[33] He developed the theme the following week:

> Those Labour MPs who voted against the Bill... certainly did so because of their objections to the methods of the Northern Ireland government.
>
> I respect their views, but there is nothing in this Bill condoning fake elections or suppression of any kind.
>
> I think the people of the North have as much right to say

they want to stay inside the Commonwealth and part of the United Kingdom as the people of the South have to say they want to be out of the Commonwealth. And as we believe in parliamentary institutions I do not see how this view can be expressed except through parliament...

I think there ought to be a commission of inquiry to deal with these questions, and in particular to examine the various Special Powers Acts in that country...

However the Bill confers great benefits on the Irish people in this country, without altering by one jot the status conferred on Ulster by the Treaty of 1921, signed by Michael Collins.

P.S. Michael Collins was a wiser and braver Irishman than are the Irish leaders who have followed him.[34]

Michael Foot's journalistic licence had gotten the better of both his sense of logic and political integrity. There was a contradiction in raising the sanctity of 'parliamentary institutions' while at the same time talking of 'undemocratic methods' and 'fake elections' employed by the Northern Irish parliamentary institution under discussion. Nor was it the case that the MPs who voted against the Bill 'certainly did so' only because of the lack of democracy within the North — what many were principally rejecting was the cementing of partition. There is little truth either in the assertion that the status of the North was not changed 'one jot' by the Ireland Act.

Foot's call for an inquiry into the Special Powers Act and his complaints about lack of democracy in the North were discussed in Cabinet during the Bill's passage through parliament. The minutes of the meeting on 12 May record:

The Cabinet was informed that a small number of government supporters had abstained from voting in the division on the second reading of the Ireland Bill the previous evening. There was some anxiety about the provision in clause 1(1)B of the Bill guaranteeing the territorial integrity of Northern Ireland, by reason of a lack of confidence in the fairness of the electoral arrangements in force in Northern Ireland. Doubts were being expressed about the wisdom of leaving the powers of veto contained in that clause in the hands of a parliament which might not fairly reflect the people's will. In the Cabinet discussion the suggestion was made that, after the Bill had been passed, the United Kingdom government might take steps to satisfy themselves that the Northern Ireland parliament was, in fact, so constituted as to reflect fairly the views of the electors. It was, however, the general view of ministers that the United Kingdom government would be ill-advised to appear to be interesting themselves in this matter, which fell under the jurisdiction of the Northern Ireland government.[35]

The Labour Cabinet's decision to turn a blind eye to what was happening in Northern Ireland was to prove crucial. It may be the case that even if the Unionists had been forced to put their house in order in 1949 the British would still have found partition, to use Jack Beattie's words, 'haunting them'. Maybe it was as impossible to reform the Northern Ireland state in 1949 as it proved twenty years later. However, one thing is certain: by extending the authority of the Northern Ireland parliament in 1949 while at the same time refusing to challenge its flouting of democracy, the Labour government was truly washing its hands in the blood which had flown and would continue to flow from partition.

The Labour dissidents on the Ireland Act were not offered reform. For daring to disagree, they were punished. Five parliamentary secretaries who had voted for the two amendments on clause 1(1)B were sacked. They included Bob Mellish, a future chief whip. The others were J.P.W. Mallalieu, F. Beswick, G. Rogers and W.R. Blyton who was Lord Pakenham's assistant in the Civil Aviation ministry. Herbert Morrison was prominent in demanding the rebels' heads.[36] Henceforth, he would be the one who 'continue to keep a protective eye on Ulster's interests in the Labour Cabinet'.[37]

Morrison's self-appointed guardianship of Unionism surfaced at the 1949 Labour Party conference in June. It was too soon after the Commons vote to have allowed affiliated organisations to forward resolutions on the Ireland Act, but three delegates did seek to raise the issue during the executive committee's report. Morrison replied on behalf of the executive and repeated what he had told the Commons: 'We are not going to coerce Northern Ireland'.[38] In reply to criticism of gerrymandering and other restrictions on civil liberty in Northern Ireland, he advised: 'That is a matter for the government and parliament of Northern Ireland,' but added that he wished, 'to warn the delegates with regards to accepting as facts everything that is said to them'.

Morrison concluded:

> It would be most unwise for us or anybody else to seek to involve the British Labour Party in internal Irish politics... we do not want to interfere with the internal politics of Ireland and, with great respect, we would like Ireland not to interfere with the internal politics of the United Kingdom... we would advise the conference that it would be inexpedient and unwise for us to be embroiled in all the excitement of internal Irish politics.

His advice was not altogether heeded. When in 1950 *Tribune* published Geoffrey Bing's pamphlet, *John Bull's Other Island*, an exposure of the lack of civil liberties in Northern Ireland, 150,000 copies were sold.[39] Fifteen years would pass before the Labour Party was forced to recognise the conditions Bing recorded in his pamphlet.

7. Inertia

When Denis Healey first stood for parliament at the end of the second world war he was heckled at one of his public meetings... by his father. 'He asked me what the Labour policy was on Ireland. I had no idea'.[1]

Healey's was not an exceptional ignorance. The passing of the 1949 Ireland Act did not attract great attention within the Labour Party. Most historians of the 1945-51 Labour government give it only a passing mention. Compared to the great controversies of the first majority Labour government — the establishment of the National Health Service, the battles over nationalisation and the start of the Cold War — Labour's Irish policy of the period has been seen as of marginal interest, at least as far as British commentators and politicians are concerned.

To Unionists in the North, Labour's attitude was especially important and would remain in their political consciousness for years to come. They had been wary of what a British Labour government might do about Ireland. The experience of 1945-51 was a reassurance. As Terence O'Neill, Unionist Prime Minister from 1963-69 has testified: 'I remember a Minister in the post-war Labour government visiting Belfast and saying to me: "We were very badly advised about Northern Ireland before the war, but today we have learnt our lesson" '.[2]

So when Labour returned to power in 1964 the Unionists had no reason to be apprehensive. On the contrary — just before Harold Wilson became the first Labour Prime Minister in 13 years, O'Neill had visited him in London — he recorded in his notes: 'When I tell him how well we were treated by the last Labour government he assures me we shall be equally well treated by the next'.[3]

Wilson's promise must have been music to Unionist ears, for there was much about their administration of the North of Ireland that was diametrically opposed to Labour's ideals. There was the discrimination against Catholics in public employment and housing; local government boundaries so arranged as to give minority Unionist populations control in councils; local government voting legislation which ensured that the mainly Protestant business community had extra votes. And a law and order policy that meant that the police, the Royal Ulster Constabulary, and their auxiliaries, the exclusively Protestant 'B' Specials, were, as one account had it, 'the military arm of the Unionist Party'.[4]

All of this and more has been adequately documented and recorded[5] and Labour's leaders were certainly not ignorant of this situation. Harold Wilson's account of the 1964-70 Labour government contains the following entry:

> On 5 August [1966] I had my most important meeting up to that time with Captain Terence O'Neill, the Prime Minister of Northern Ireland. The Home Secretary and I had a private lunch with him, then went on talking well into the afternoon. Captain O'Neill had already made more progress in a matter of two or three years in attacking problems of discrimination and human rights than all his Stormont predecessors had made in more than forty years...
>
> There was no doubt about his courage and resolve. Roy Jenkins and I agreed not to press him further for the next few months.[6]

What exactly was this 'progress' Wilson mentions? Certainly, O'Neill had aroused anger and suspicion among Unionists by meeting Irish premier Sean Lemass in 1965. And by visiting a number of Catholic institutions, schools, convents and the like, O'Neill had stepped where no Northern Irish premier had gone before. But these gestures, significant enough in the Northern Ireland context, did not materially alter the inferior treatment meted out to Catholics.

The Northern Ireland Labour Party, sister organisation of the British Labour Party, made a general judgement in late 1965:

> No attempt has been made by the Northern Ireland government to knit the community together; there has been no electoral reforms, no review of electoral boundaries... there is to be no ombudsman... not merely has Captain O'Neill dashed the hopes he himself raised, he has added a new bitterness and disappointment to the grievances of the minority.[7]

Other doubts can be cast on Wilson's version of his August 1966 meeting with O'Neill. The Unionist leader himself, in his account of the discussion, wrote that Wilson and Jenkins asked him 'Why are you pursuing a policy which is so unpopular with the Protestants when you could, for instance, have decided not to meet Mr Lemass?' The Labour Ministers, says O'Neill, 'merely intended to have a talk in general terms'.[8]

Wilson's memory can also be questioned over the next meeting he had with O'Neill, in January 1967. O'Neill, claimed Wilson, had 'pressed on with domestic reforms, particularly in the field of local government, electoral law and housing'.[9]

Again, this is simply not true. The assessment of life for the minority in Northern Ireland made in April 1967 by Labour MPs Stanley Orme, Maurice Miller and Paul Rose is more accurate:

> Allegations of discrimination in housing allocations were examined. There is little doubt that this exists on a wide scale... Discrimination on political and religious grounds is alleged and substantiated by figures previously provided by the Northern Ireland Labour Party, and other sources, and confirmed by all those with whom this was discussed... the electoral franchise which excludes 250,000 voters from local government elections, and allows business and company votes (up to six) is an anomaly in the UK.[10]

Orme, Miller and Rose offered these conclusions in a file submitted to the government after a three-day visit to Northern Ireland. Their report, which demanded a Royal Commission on civil liberties in Northern Ireland, is of great significance. It is evidence that the government was forewarned about the storm which broke when the civil rights movement took to the streets in 1968. But knowing there were many things rotten in the state of Northern Ireland and doing anything about them were two different things. 'Any politician who wants to get involved with Ulster,' Wilson is reputed to have said in 1964, 'ought to have his head examined'.[11] Or, as James Callaghan admitted when he became Home Secretary and responsible for Northern Ireland in December 1967: 'I had no occasion to seek more work or to go out and look at the problems of Northern Ireland, unless they forced themselves upon me'.[12]

Eventually the question of civil liberties in Northern Ireland was indeed 'forced upon' Callaghan. What is perhaps most remarkable is just how long it took for pressure to be forthcoming. There are, however, reasons for this. In Northern Ireland the opposition to the Unionists was mainly channelled into the staid conservatism of the Nationalist Party or the fruitless IRA 'border campaign' of 1956-62. Both were ineffectual, allowing the Unionists a comparatively easy ride. In addition, O'Neill and his colleagues continued to be shielded by the convention that Northern Ireland should not be discussed at Westminster. The topic surfaced in the House of Commons only rarely. One instance was in June 1955 when the Tory government proposed that a by-election in Mid-Ulster be declared null and void because the successful candidate Tom Mitchell, a member of the IRA, was serving a ten-year jail sentence. Sidney Silverman led 67 Labour MPs in the vote against, but the proposal was easily carried. Yet the willingness of so many Labour MPs to vote against showed a potential in the Labour Party for a more progressive stance on Ireland.

It was ten years after the Mitchell vote before such interests were awakened with the formation of the Campaign of Democracy in Ulster (CDU) after a meeting in the House of Commons.

The CDU was different from earlier Irish lobbies in that it did not seek to challenge either the partition of Ireland or British control of the North. Indeed, it sought to make Westminster more responsible for Northern Ireland. The CDU aimed to break the Commons' silence on Ireland, pointing out that the 1920 Government of Ireland Act endowed Westminster with 'supreme authority' over 'all persons, matters and things' in Northern Ireland.

The CDU's intention was to highlight the abuses of power exercised by the Unionists. In doing so it worked closely with the Dungannon-based Campaign for Social Justice.

Paul Rose was the CDU's first chairman. A year earlier he had successfully contested the Manchester constituency of Blackley in the 1964 general election and his interest in Northern Ireland stemmed from a discussion he had had with Irish constituents in Manchester in 1962. The CDU's secretary was Paddy Byrne, a member of Hammersmith Labour Party. Other members of the Labour Party who showed an active interest in the early days of the CDU included MPs Eric Heffer, Stan Orme and Kevin McNamara.

CDU association and interest were not restricted to Labour Party members — John Pardoe of the Liberals was one of those involved — but it was on the Labour Party, and MPs in particular, that the CDU focused its attention. The most obvious explanation for this is that Labour's ideological traditions suggested the party would be more open than others to arguments on civil liberties. Another factor was that Labour was now in government. A third was Labour's wafer-thin parliamentary majority from 1964-66, with drew attention to the 12 seats held by the Ulster Unionists who always voted with the Tories. CDU members hoped this would persuade Labour MPs to study what the Unionists were up to in Northern Ireland more closely.

Paul Rose quoted two further reasons for the CDU orientation towards the Labour Party. One was 'an increasingly aware rank and file [of the Labour Party] concerned at the grievances of the minority in Northern Ireland';[13] the other was 'the new intake of Labour MPs concerned at this denial of their deals in their own backyard'.

The CDU gained impressive support, at least on paper. More than 100 prominent sponsors included Labour MPs David Owen, Michael Foot, Roy Hattersley, Brian Walden, Reg Prentice and Ian Mikardo.[14] Yet apart from producing some hard-hitting and informative propaganda, the CDU achieved little. It had no discernible effect on the Labour government.

Alice Bacon, one of the Home Office Ministers in the pre-1968 period, was, like Harold Wilson, rather over-impressed by Terence O'Neill's endeavours. But it would be wrong to blame one or two leading members of the government for the rebuffs encountered by the CDU. The attitude of allowing a seemingly sleeping dog to lie was a general one. Roy Jenkins warned Paul Rose that 'Ireland had been the political graveyard of many a politician',[15] while Chief Whip Ted Short spoke of 'religious controversies in their constituencies' as a reason for Labour MPs not being more active over Ireland.[16]

The impression is one of active disinterest, maintaining the tradition of earlier years: the 'it is not our business' view of the first two decades of the twentieth century; the attitude of 1946 that 'there was plenty of trouble in the world already' without fishing in Irish pools.

Even after 5 October 1968, when the first powerful warning shot was fired, the Labour government did its best to continue with its policy of abstentionism over Ireland. The occasion was the bloody baptism of the civil rights movement when the Royal Ulster Constabulary (RUC) savagely attacked a demonstration in Derry. The event was witnessed by TV cameras. Suddenly, Northern Ireland became news. On 22 October, Paul Rose asked Wilson to transfer control of the RUC to Westminster. The Prime Minister declined. Instead, as he has since put it: 'I took the opportunity of paying one in a long series of tributes to what Captain O'Neill had carried through in the way of liberalisation in the face of great difficulties'.[17]

There was still little practical evidence of this 'liberalisation', but the publicity the civil rights cause attracted after the street clashes on 5 October ensured that some correction in Unionist policies became inevitable. When Wilson, Callaghan and Alice Bacon met O'Neill and two of his right wing critics within the Unionist Cabinet, William Craig and Brian Faulkner, the Labour leaders pressed for reforms. If these were not forthcoming, Wilson warned, then Westminster would directly intervene, although, the Prime Minister was to recall, 'none of us wanted that'.[18] According to Callaghan, Wilson threatened: 'We might have to apply sanctions such as reconsidering the financial arrangements between the two countries, or even changing their constitutional relationship'.[19] Wilson was even more explicit when he reported the meeting to parliament the following day: 'If Captain O'Neill were thrown over, or what he was trying to do were thrown over, by extremists, we should ourselves need to consider a fundamental reappraisal of our relations with Northern Ireland'.[20]

This was waving a very big stick, and O'Neill agreed to introduce a number of reforms. These increased the right wing opposition within O'Neill's own party. After an inconclusive Northern Ireland general election, and with further defections from his own party and the rising demands of the civil rights movement, O'Neill resigned in April 1969. It was a victory for the Unionist right wing, but it led to no 'fundamental reappraisal' of the Labour government's relations with Northern Ireland. Wilson's threats of November 1968 proved mere bluff.

What the overthrow of O'Neill did produce from Harold

Wilson was the formation of a top secret Northern Ireland Cabinet Committee. He selected Callaghan, Healey, Roy Jenkins, Foreign Secretary Michael Stewart, Lord Gardiner, the government's senior legal adviser, and Richard Crossman, Minister for Social Services.

Crossman's inclusion was at his own insistence. At a Cabinet meeting on 24 April, just after the Northern Ireland Committee had been established without him, Crossman asked for a brief Cabinet discussion on Northern Ireland. 'On everything, I got prevaricating answers', Crossman was to recall. 'Harold did not want this to come to Cabinet'.[21] Crossman expressed his view of Labour policy in his diary three days later: 'We are being dragged closer and closer to the precipice of protecting the Orangemen in Ireland'.[22] It seems likely he was added to the Northern Ireland Committee by Wilson on 29 April to stop him asking awkward questions in full Cabinet.

The Labour government's Northern Ireland policy was now shrouded in secrecy, confined to discussion among the most senior members of the Cabinet. According to Tony Benn, speaking at a fringe meeting at the Labour Party conference in October 1980, there were only two occasions from 1966-70 and from 1974-79, the period of the subsequent Labour government, on which Northern Ireland was fully discussed in full Cabinet: when the troops went in, and during the Ulster Workers' Council strike in 1974.[23]

The Crossman diaries testify to two other discussions besides those mentioned by Benn, whose confusion is understandable because, again according to Crossman, the record of at least one of these discussions did not appear in subsequent Cabinet minutes.[24] Crossman makes it clear that the foundations of the wall of silence around Northern Ireland which was to be so manifest in British politics in the 1970s was laid in the 1960s.

The formation of the Northern Ireland Committee suggested that the government was at least beginning to take the issue seriously. Yet those accounts of the Committee's workings which have surfaced imply that the discussions were largely technical or concerned with limiting direct government intervention, an obsession particularly relevant from April 1969 as recognition dawned that British troops might have to be sent in.

Crossman wrote: 'I found the Committee had already come to the conclusion that it was impossible to evade British responsibility if there was civil war or widespread rioting. Strictly speaking, the police in Ireland or the government can ask for British troops to come'.[25] At the end of July a Cabinet meeting gave Wilson and Callaghan authority to send in troops if O'Neill's successor, James Chichester-Clark, asked for them.

Labour's main aim was still to avoid such an option. 'We were debating whether we should intervene, but hoping and praying that we should not have to,' Callaghan has written.[26] To avoid biting the bullet, all sorts of concessions were made to the Unionists. When it was suggested that the Orange Order parades on 12 July be banned, Callaghan objected on the grounds that it could topple Chichester-Clark. Two days and nights of rioting followed the marches. To tackle any further outbreaks against the next Orange march in Derry on 12 August, the Cabinet agreed at the end of July to allow the RUC to use CS gas, as an alternative to sending in the troops. With chilling accuracy the new Chief Whip Bob Mellish, who had been one of the 1949 rebels, predicted: 'But if we do this, won't British troops be engaged anyway and won't it be a bloody scandal and won't our own people be against it, and won't we find ourselves with British troops fighting on the side of Ulster reactionaries?'[27]

The reference to fighting on the side of the 'reactionary' Unionists was made because the Cabinet — and especially its Northern Ireland Committee — had been discussing whether the government would have to take direct responsibility for the six counties in the event of the troops going in. Again the urge was to avoid this option. Roy Jenkins warned: 'If there is one thing I have learnt it is that the British cannot run Ireland',[28] and another Cabinet member later confided to the *Sunday Times*, 'In practice our policy therefore amounted to doing anything which could avoid direct rule'.[29]

Outside the Cabinet discussions, Wilson was playing a different tune. He leaked a story to the *Financial Times*[30] which reported on 6 August: 'British troops would be used to restore law and order in Ulster only if the Northern Ireland government first agreed to surrender its political authority to Westminster.' It was another bluff, and again it was called. The troops were sent in on 14 August after three days of rioting by Catholics in

Derry's Bogside — but the Unionist government stayed in office. As Lawrence Orr, leader of the Unionist MPs at Westminster, commented privately: 'We're getting the troops and we're getting them without strings'.[31]

Subsequent mythology has grown up that the Labour government dispatched troops to Northern Ireland in August 1969 to protect the helpless Catholics against Orange mobs, or to 'keep the two sides apart'. Neither was the case. The troops went in because the Bogsiders had defeated the Unionists' police. As Callaghan has testified: 'The police were dog-tired and unable to hold the exposed position they had taken up'.[32] His official statement explaining the arrival of the troops expanded his views:

> The government of Northern Ireland has informed the United Kingdom government that as a result of the severe and prolonged rioting in Londonderry it has no alternative but to ask for the assistance of the troops at present stationed in Northern Ireland to prevent a breakdown of law and order...
>
> The United Kingdom government has received assessment of the situation from the Northern Ireland government and the GOC Northern Ireland, and has agreed to this request in order to restore order in Londonderry with the greatest possible speed.[33]

In other words, the troops came to the aid of the Unionist government. This was recognised at the time. The day the troops went in Crossman thought: 'We would find ourselves supporting the Orangemen in Northern Ireland.'[34] The signs that such a situation was materialising were evident at the Cabinet meeting on 19 August. Denis Healey warned: 'We must only push Chichester-Clark as far as he wants to go' and Healey and Callaghan expressed the view that 'our whole interest is to work through the Protestant government. The Protestants are the majority and we can't afford to alienate them'.[35]

There was nothing original in such advice. Although Harold Wilson was later to write that Derry in August 1969 'was the culmination of nearly fifty years of the unimaginative inertia and repression by successive and unchallenged — and because of Ulster's history, unchallengeable — Ulster Unionist government',[36] the Wilson administration of the sixties was part of that inertia. The rejection of the lobbying of the CDU, the sowing of illusions in O'Neill and Chichester-Clark and the bluffs that failed were all apart of a general apathy that allowed the Northern Ireland problem to fester and grow. Wilson wrote: 'In this, as in so many other issues the Labour government had to act at the eleventh hour after years of neglect'.[37] But his own Cabinet shared that neglect and, eleventh hour or not, had spent five years watching the clock ticking and done nothing.

Whatever the failures of Labour policies during those first five years in power, their decisions of 1969 were a total disaster. First, the move to send in the troops; then allowing the Unionist government to continue. It is ironic that even Terence O'Neill found the latter decision rather cowardly: 'The imposition of direct rule should, in my opinion, have come in August or September 1969,' he later wrote,[38] adding, 'Time alone will show whether this was one of the missed opportunities of Irish history. Certainly what has happened since could not have been worse'.[39]

What did happen immediately after the deployment of troops, first to Derry and then to Belfast, was a meeting of British and Northern Irish government representatives in Downing Street on 19 August. The 'Declaration' by the UK government that emerged was drafted by Wilson. The first point read:

> The United Kingdom government reaffirm that nothing which has happened in recent weeks in Northern Ireland derogates from the clear pledges made by successive United Kingdom governments that Northern Ireland should not cease to be part of the United Kingdom without the consent of the parliament of Northern Ireland. The border is not an issue.[40]

It was true that in August 1969 the border was not an issue, though it would become the central one within two years and remain so for at least a decade. The chief reason was the failure to meet the aspirations of the civil rights movement. There were reforms, which increased in scope after August 1969. The local government franchise was extended to one person, one vote. Discrimination in council housing allocation was ended, the 'B' Specials were disbanded and an ombudsman was appointed. But the changes were insufficient to pacify the Catholic community. After a brief honeymoon with the British troops, Catholics saw them, as Bob Mellish had predicted, 'fighting on the side of

Orange reactionaries'.

There was never really any chance that the Westminster government would disband the Unionist parliament at Stormont in 1969, for Labour had too long a history of taking the soft option on Northern Ireland. There were Labour backbenchers who suspected that the hurried reforms were too late. Paul Rose told the Labour conference held a month after the troops went in:

> We were told by Unionists when we talked about discrimination in housing, employment and other bodies that this was a complete falsehood, that we had been duped by the Republicans and extremists. Five years ago we asked for a Royal Commission into Northern Ireland; now we have several commissions, but they have all come too late.
>
> When I first moved an amendment to the Parliamentary Commissioner Bill to extend it to Northern Ireland, I was told it was impracticable and unconstitutional, and that we do not legislate for Northern Ireland... When this very reform was announced a year later by the Prime Minister, it came at a time when, unfortunately, it was too late to soothe passions and was ineffectual in diffusing tensions.[41]

Rose went on to complain that the Special Powers Act was still on the statute book, the RUC still needed to be reformed and a 'massive injection of economic help' was necessary. Such scepticism was uncommon in Labour Party ranks. The 1969 conference was the first time for nearly fifty years that the Labour Party had debated Ireland, yet the atmosphere was headily optimistic. The reason was the impact Callaghan had made during his visits to the North after the Downing Street Declaration. 'The ten days have been completely overshadowed by Jim Callaghan's visit to Ireland', Crossman noted in his diary entry for 3 September 1969.

> He had gone, he had seen, he had conquered. He had got the confidence of the Protestants, the confidence of the Catholics, and he dominated the news on the radio for three days. Frankly, it is the only successful diplomatic episode in these five years of a Labour government, a one man success story.

Crossman's enthusiasm was reflected at the party conference. An emergency resolution, moved by Brentford and

Chiswick Constituency Labour Party commended: 'The ability with which the Home Secretary brought all the responsible leaders together during his visit to Northern Ireland'.[42] MP Willie Hamilton thought: 'The conference should not lose the opportunity for complimenting Jim Callaghan on the way he has handled the problem of Ulster',[43] a remark which was applauded. Concluding the debate, conference chairperson Eileen White declared: 'I am sure that we are very grateful to Jim for what he is doing in this problem'.[44]

Callaghan's warm reception at the conference reflected the welcome he had been given in Northern Ireland during his 27-29 August visit. The highlight had been an impromptu speech delivered to the Bogsiders. Callaghan later recalled: 'I went on to say that I was not on anyone's side — Protestant or Catholic. But I was on the side of those whoever they were and whatever community they might belong to, who were deprived of freedom and justice'.[45]

There were noble sentiments, in dramatic contrast to fifty years of British political disinterest in Northern Irish civil liberties, and untypical of a Labour government which had, by the autumn of 1969, long discarded the socialist rhetoric which had propelled it into office in 1964. Callaghan's popularity at the 1969 Labour conference was fuelled by a feeling that, at least on Northern Ireland, Labour was talking good socialism.

Eamonn McCann, then leader of the left wing of the Derry civil rights movement, has explained the warmth of Callaghan's reception in the city:

> Callaghan... had been very popular with the people as a whole, not because of any personal qualities but because, if the arrival of the British Army symbolised our physical victory over the RUC, Callaghan's appearance symbolised the political defeat of the Unionist Party. They were no longer calling the shots. The boss himself had arrived to put them in their place.[46]

But there were strict limitations on how far Callaghan was prepared to go. As he has written: 'At the back of my mind, of course, I still did not want Britain to get more embroiled in Northern Ireland than we had to'.[47] So he rejected McCann and others in the Derry Defence Committee when they demanded the abolition of Stormont and the repeal of the Special Powers Act.

When he arrived in triumph at the Labour Party conference, Callaghan showed the same reticence. He asked for and won remittance of a resolution which 'calls upon the British government, if necessary to use its full powers under the Government of Ireland Act'. Implementation rather than remission, argued Callaghan, would have meant the British government exercising more authority than was desired. Instead: 'I believe we must go to the limit in allowing, encouraging, spurring on the Northern Ireland government to solve these particular problems that have arisen under their jurisdiction'.[48] On the Special Powers Act Callaghan, on behalf of Labour's national executive, accepted a resolution which demanded 'immediate legislation to abolish powers of detention without trial'. However, he added the caveat: 'But I am not going to guarantee to the conference in accepting this resolution that I undertake also to introduce legislation immediately to this effect'.[49]

The general tenor of Callaghan's speech was friendly, confident and full of good intentions. He appealed to Catholics and Protestants to work together and expressed the hope that 'out of this evil could come good'. The only alternative offered to the conference came from supporters of the dogmatic left-wing *Militant* newspaper, who called on the trade unions in Ireland to organise 'joint defence committees',[50] in the belief that Catholic and Protestant workers would be easily united if the prospect of red-blooded socialism became feasible. Their utopian resolution was defeated.

The conference belonged to Callaghan. He ended his speech with a flourish:

> This movement should commit itself, not just to solving the short-term temporary problems, getting the civil rights through and then pushing it under the rug, but to trying to ensure that relations between everyone living in the north and south of that island are lifted onto a new plane so that they can all live in peace and prosperity.[51]

Nine years later, when Callaghan looked back on his stewardship of Northern Ireland, he hummed a different Labour Party song. He acknowledged that 'the Catholics at that time were in a position of very great inferiority' but maintained: 'I think it would be fair to say that I over-estimated the civil rights aspect'.[52]

His retrospective judgement came when another Labour government was going through its most pro-Unionist period and Callaghan's stark denigration of the civil rights cause must be seen in that context. Yet his erroneous aside contained an element of unconscious truth. For what was mistaken was Labour's apparent expectation in 1969 that pledging reforms would bring sweetness and light to Northern Ireland. It was never that simple. The next time a Labour conference discussed Northern Ireland — in 1971 — this was beginning to dawn on them. By then, one delegate was telling the conference: 'Reforms have come too late',[53] while another insisted: 'The border is an issue, always has been an issue, and will continue to be an issue'.[54]

Between the 1969 and 1971 conferences Labour had lost a general election in June 1970 and Callaghan, who at least had shown energy in dealing with Northern Ireland, had been replaced as Minister responsible by the docile Tory Reggie Maudling. Maudling's attitude was summed up by the famous remark he made on a jet leaving Belfast: 'For God's sake bring me a large Scotch. What a bloody awful country'.[55]

But the change in British government personnel responsible for Northern Ireland was not pivotal to future developments there. Callaghan admitted: 'The change of government made it easy for trouble-makers to convince the Catholic community that the British government policy had changed. This was not so; what was true was that the Conservative government was failing to give guidance to the men on the spot'.[56]

It was correct to assess the differences between the two parties as minimal. Wilson's Northern Ireland Committee had sought to take political discussion away from the Cabinet and party generally, but it had acted in close consultation with the Tory opposition. Callaghan had had frequent discussions with his Shadow, Quintin Hogg, who, in Callaghan's words, 'always gave me unstinting support in the House of Commons'.[57]

Thus was born the Tory-Labour bi-partisan approach to Northern Ireland. Under its protective umbrella even the insipid Maudling received, as Callaghan put it, 'a favourable wind from the Labour Party'.[58] In 1979, referring to the bipartisanship, Wilson was to recall 'frequent meetings (on Northern Ireland) between the two party leaders in the Prime Minister's room behind the Speaker's chair', as a consequence of which there was 'in the past 16 years only one party division on Ulster in the Commons'.[59]

This 'broad support for both Labour and Conservative governments... from the Opposition of the day' led to 'the formation and execution of a consistent policy by Britain',[60] according to Callaghan. It also meant such a policy would inevitably be timid and conservative.

The pursuit of bipartisanship became almost an end in itself. From 1964-69 it had ruled out the type of radical measures which would have been necessary if there was to have been even the remotest chance of an amelioration of the situation. As Callaghan has confirmed: 'Each government was very conscious of the need to frame its policies so as to carry the Opposition with it'.[61] Bipartisanship reaped its bitterest fruit with the introduction of internment in August 1971 by a Unionist Stormont led by Brian Faulkner and endorsed by the British Tories under Edward Heath.

Imprisonment without trial was ordered under the terms of the same Special Powers Act the Labour Party conference of 1969 had disowned, but criticism of the operation by the Party's parliamentary leaders was muted. Callaghan's only complaint was that internment had not been accompanied by a political initiative.[62] Wilson told the Commons: 'The House will need much more evidence than it has had if it is to be convinced that the dividend in terms of security deriving from the arrest of key criminals is an adequate return for aggravating tensions and inter-communal hostility'.[63]

These were shots across the Tory bows over a matter of detail, rather than principle. At the end of the emergency debate on Northern Ireland in September 1971 Labour officially abstained, although a considerable number of Labour MPs did vote against the government.

The party outside Westminster took a more critical attitude. Its representatives and those of the Northern Ireland Labour Party and the (Southern) Irish Labour Party met in London in September and declared: 'It was agreed that the introduction of internment in Northern Ireland had alienated wide sections of the community, was unacceptable and that no realistic solution could even be envisaged without an end to internment and the release of detainees held without trial'.[64] A specific call for an immediate end to internment came a few weeks later at the Labour Party conference.

The atmosphere there was markedly different from the enthusiasm displayed during the Northern Ireland debate two years earlier. Gone was the sense of achievement and purpose; frustration had taken its place. The left was annoyed at the Parliamentary Party's ambiguity on internment, while the party leaders wriggled and squirmed over explanations over why they couldn't agree with amendments calling for its ending for the imposition of direct rule, and support for a united Ireland.

Kevin McNamara led the attack on internment with a fierce denunciation of the Tory government and, by heavy implication, the Parliamentary Labour Party's (PLP) acquiescence to it. Callaghan and the recently appointed parliamentary spokesman on Northern Ireland, Merlyn Rees, defended the PLP's stand. In an anguished speech, Rees stopped short of condemning internment out of hand. His worry was that 'it has not worked'. His demand was vague: 'We must press the government to deal with internment, to deal with the situation'.[65]

Callaghan was less timid. He agreed that internment was a 'loathsome weapon' but, as he later wrote: 'I reminded the delegates... we had to reconcile the principles we all held with ensuring that people could go about their lives without fear of violence'.[66]

It was a dubious argument, even on the 'practical' grounds referred to in parliament by Wilson. The reality was that internment had produced the greatest upsurge in violence the Northern Ireland state had ever seen.

Nevertheless, Callaghan convinced the conference. The amendments were heavily defeated. The substantive resolution calling for 'equal rights to all citizens' and 'a peaceful and just method of removing the border' was remitted. Bipartisanship had enveloped the Labour Party conference.

A month later, a large crack in the wall of all-party unanimity appeared, by courtesy of an unexpected quarter — Harold Wilson.

He made his dramatic announcement in the House of Commons on 25 November, having just returned from a 36-hour visit to Northern Ireland in which he crammed 32 meetings with politicians, church leaders, security chiefs and local community representatives. He did not encounter any member of the IRA, saying: 'I would not meet any men who sought to change the existing order by violence'.[67] He had also spent some time in the South of Ireland meeting political leaders.

Wilson told the Commons of his impressions. First, he recalled how, when the Army had gone into the Catholic ghettos, they had been cheered. 'Today,' Wilson reported, those who had been part of the welcome had told him: 'The troops are fighting two wars — the IRA and what we call the residents of the Catholic ghettos'. The Labour leader commented: 'I believe that to be totally untrue, but the important fact in the situation... is that so many people believe it'.[68] Wilson's was the first public admission by a leading British politician that perhaps the Army in Northern Ireland did not always behave as delicately as it might. So what was the Labour leader's solution to the Irish problem?

'First,' Wilson said, 'violence must cease and be seen to cease' — a bland enough proposal. Then came the bombshell. Wilson called for the establishment of a constitutional commission made up of representatives of the governments of Britain, the North and the South of Ireland. The terms of reference of this commission would be 'involved in agreeing on the constitution of a united Ireland'.

It had been little more than two years since Wilson, when Prime Minister, had issued a declaration insisting: 'The border is not an issue'. Here he was asserting that it should be removed. Wilson went on to say this all-Ireland constitution should come into effect 15 years after it was drawn up. The Labour leader was quite clear that the British government should declare its intention to leave Ireland by the mid-1980s.

The other proposals in Wilson's 15-point plan determined the process of withdrawal. He said 'internment should cease as soon as the necessary conditions exist for improvement in confidence'. He suggested the constitution of a united Ireland should include 'safeguards for the rights of minorities'; the South of Ireland should rejoin the Commonwealth; there should be an optional oath of allegiance to the British monarch in the parliament of the united Ireland. In the interim period, the Northern Irish government should contain representatives of the minority while the new Ireland should have British-standard education and social services, which Britian would help finance.

Wilson's plan resembled what Labour had proposed fifty years earlier. However, compared to what the Party had been saying since 1969, this was all totally new. The leader of the Labour Party was calling for a united Ireland whether the Unionists in the North liked it or not. What price bipartisanship now?

8. Bipartisanship

Harold Wilson's call in November 1971 for British withdrawal and Irish unity within 15 years was never endorsed by the Labour Party. Instead, at the 1972 party conference, delegates accepted a statement from the National Executive Committee (NEC) calling for political parties in Northern Ireland and Westminster to set up talks, which Southern Irish parties could join later. These discussions would 'consider' Wilson's 15-point programme... as well as 'any other proposals put forward by other parties'.[1]

A resolution calling for 'a declaration of support in principle for a united Ireland' was remitted on the advice of the NEC, on whose behalf Shirley Williams told the conference: 'We believe...that eventually a united Ireland is the best framework for the future, but... we do not believe such a solution can or should be imposed'.[2]

The Labour leader's support for Irish unity had not been conditional on the agreement of the Unionist majority in the North. At the 1972 conference both Williams and Merlyn Rees, while generally endorsing the Wilson plan, insisted it could only be achieved with Unionist consent.

In stressing the difference between Wilson's ideas in November 1971 and the NEC statement of October 1972 it is not suggested that this led to an internal party squabble. Events over the intervening 11 months had changed the political circumstances in Northern Ireland. Wilson had already gone back on one promise made in November 1971, when he had vowed never to meet 'any men who sought to change the existing order by violence'. In March and June 1972, in the company of Merlyn Rees, he had secret meetings in Dublin and Buckinghamshire with leaders of the Provisional IRA. Although nothing concrete came from these encounters, they at least show that

Labour's leaders recognised that if the IRA were part of the war they should also be part of the peace. It was an acknowledgement which testified to the rapidly deteriorating situation in Northern Ireland.

The greatest shock-wave came on 30 January 1972 in Derry when the British Army shot and killed 14 anti-internment demonstrators in what became known as 'Bloody Sunday'. Despite the more questioning and flexible approach Labour's front bench at Westminster had been showing on Irish policy, Bloody Sunday saw no collective protest from the Labour parliamentarians. The Heath government ordered an immediate inquiry, to be conducted by a High Court judge. Discussion of the events in Derry on 30 January was declared sub judice until Lord Widgery reported. When he did so, his finds were transparently biased. He accused the IRA of engaging the British Army in a military conflict, but produced no evidence that any of the dead had been armed. Not one soldier had received any injury and no ammunition allegedly fired by the IRA was produced. Yet the Labour Party in parliament swallowed the Widgery Report whole. 'There tragic events belong in the past', Callaghan told the Commons.

> They took place when there was a divided responsibility for security and when it is fair to say that very heavy pressure was brought to bear upon the Army commanders to step up their attitude... the description of Lord Widgery demonstrates the bankruptcy of the old policy and the need for a new one which has now superceded the old one. The Prime Minister asks for the combined support of the House. He has it.[3]

There was a powerful reason why the Labour Party could not be too critical of the government's grateful acceptance of the Widgery findings. By then, Ted Heath had done what Wilson and Callaghan had refused to do: he had suspended Stormont and imposed direct rule. This was the substance of the 'new policy' referred to by Callaghan in the debate on Widgery.

The 'new policy' made a number of concessions to Wilson's 15-point plan of November 1971. In particular, point 11 of Wilson's programme, that the Northern Ireland government 'should include representatives of minority views', was a key feature of Heath's strategy after March 1972. A further nod in Wilson's direction was the acceptance that what was happening in the United Kingdom's six most westerly counties did, after all, have an 'Irish dimension'.

This became evident in the Sunningdale Agreement of December 1973. Elections to a new Assembly to replace direct rule had already taken place. The Tory government had also managed to persuade a section of the Unionists, led by Brian Faulkner, the mainly Catholic Social Democratic and Labour Party and the most moderate of the Unionist parties, Alliance, to form a power-sharing executive which would head the Assembly. The Sunningdale Agreement, in which the new executive, the British government and the Irish government participated, also proposed a Council of Ireland.

It was to be two-tier. The higher body would comprise government ministers from the North and South, the lower grouping would be members elected on a fifty/fifty basis by the Assembly and the Irish parliament. The powers of the Council were to be severely restricted.

It was a proposal similar to that agreed at the time of the partition of Ireland, but there is no doubt that the Heath measures were a qualitative change from what had gone before. Elements of the old policy stayed, such as the continuation of internment (although some internees were released), but overall Sunningdale envisaged a Northern Ireland in which the Unionists' monopoly of political power would no longer be permitted.

It had taken Bloody Sunday and an intensive military campaign by the Provisional IRA to produce Sunningdale. The irony was that it had transpired under a Conservative government. The Sunningdale agreement might have had its theoretical precursor in Wilson's 15 points, and an all-Ireland council had certainly been suggested by Callaghan as early as March 1971, but these proposals had been made by Labour leaders out of office. When Wilson and Callaghan had held the power to face up to the Unionists, they had proved less courageous than Heath.

During the years of the Heath government few serious challenges to bipartisanship were mounted by Labour. An NEC statement agreed by the 1972 party conference had called for the repeal of the Special Powers Act, 'so that internment without trial will end'. This was a reaffirmation of a similar NEC call in December 1971, but such demands were still not unconditional. At the 1972 conference Shirley Williams was speaking for the

NEC when she distanced herself from the immediate ending of internment and proposed instead a judicial commission to examine how it could be ended.

The more substantial opposition in Britain to internment came from outside the Labour Party. The declining CDU had been replaced by the Anti-Internment League (AIL). Groups to the far left of the Labour Party, notably the International Socialists and the International Marxist Group, had a strong influence on the AIL, which had support primarily in the student and Irish communities.

The AIL was happy to keep its distance from both the leadership and the rank and file of the Labour Party. The feeling was mutual. A few constituency Labour Parties endeavoured to keep the Labour Party's Irish conscience alive, but these were mostly in places like Coventry where a large Irish community had close ties with the labour movement. Jock Stallard, Paul Rose, Kevin McNamara and a few other Labour MPs continued to be more critical of internment than their parliamentary leaders, but after Sunningdale the support they could expect in the Commons from their backbench colleagues declined.

When the Tory government fell in 1974, Sunningdale had still to prove itself. During Heath's last year in office, James Callaghan warned the Protestant community of his reaction if they vetoed the plan.

> As long as Britain is satisfied that the majority of the population accepts the final sovereignty of the Westminster parliament, then it will unquestionably hold its responsibilities to the majority on the border question... But I cannot conclude without saying that a new situation would arise if there was intransigence among the majority of Northern politicians elected to the Assembly. If at any time, the Assembly and the Executive should be made unworkable through a deliberate refusal by the majority to play their part, then in my judgement the United Kingdom would be entitled to reconsider her position and her pledges on all matters... So, if by sabotage of the political structure of Northern Ireland, the majority deliberately contracted out, then Britain should feel morally free to reconsider the link between herself and Northern Ireland, the provision of troops to Northern Ireland and the financial subsidy to the province.[4]

Strong words, but those reading them at the time might

have recalled the empty threat made by Harold Wilson during his first term of office when he had warned of 'a fundamental reappraisal of our relations with Northern Ireland' in the event of Terence O'Neill being overthrown by the Unionist right.

The seriousness of Callaghan and the rest of Labour's parliamentary leadership was soon tested. Within ten weeks of Labour's victory in the February 1974 general election, the Ulster Workers Council called a general strike. Its aim was to destroy Sunningdale, bring down the power-sharing executive and kill the Council of Ireland at birth.

The strike brought an unqualified victory for the Loyalists. Enough evidence has emerged to show that Northern Ireland Secretary, Merlyn Rees, and the rest of the Cabinet acted with little resolve and less courage.[5] The British Army was used sparingly, only rarely moving essential supplies or breaking up the intimidation used to maintain the strike by the paramilitary Ulster Defence Association, who, with their masks and clubs, were a powerful persuasion against strike-breaking.

There were limitations on what any British government could have done. For one thing, there were doubts as to how far the Army could be relied on to act against the Protestants. Writing after the event in the magazine of the right-wing Tory Monday Club, an Army officer maintained that the government had decided to used troops to smash the strike but the Army had refused.[6] Another giant hurdle was that the strike did reflect the political views of the Protestant majority in Northern Ireland. In the February 1974 general election all the eleven Unionist seats were won by anti-Sunningdale candidates.

Nevertheless, Paul Rose's view that Rees had a 'failure of nerve'[7] remains an acceptable judgement. The Northern Ireland Secretary's comment after his defeat was explicit: 'There is a new situation now which we must take account of. We have seen the rise of Ulster nationalism'.[8]

What of Callaghan's threat that the link with Britain would be up for grabs should the Protestant majority wreck Sunningdale? The immediate evidence after the UWC strike was that yet another Labour bluff had been called. Direct rule was reimposed and Rees began planning for a Northern Ireland-elected convention which would be charged with hammering out a new solution. There were no great expectations over that and by the time

Labour's annual conference came around in the autumn of 1974 a sense of hopelessness was there for all to see. Rees told the delegates:

> The problem of Ireland had defeated the men and women of this country and we bear many of the burdens and mistakes of that time... There will never be a simple solution to the problems of Northern Ireland. We have a responsibility for Northern Ireland. There is no other government there. The government of the South doesn't want it.[9]

On behalf of Labour's national executive Shirley Williams was slightly more forthright. 'In Northern Ireland we have inherited an historical tragedy. We are paying the price for three centuries of past imperialism'.[10] But judgements on the past did not produce a prescription for the future, either from Williams or the conference. Few resolutions had been submitted on Northern Ireland and the debate itself was finished quickly with only five speakers allowed. The call for an immediate end to internment was again rejected. 'It is our aim to end detention,' Rees stated, but 'I am not going to put the lives of civilians at risk for a political whim. I have to face the reality'.[11]

For those words, Rees received a round of applause. Shirley Williams was equally sober about the Prevention of Terrorism Act (PTA), which the government had just rushed through parliament, in response to the Provisionals' bombing campaign in England. Its powers, described as 'draconian' by Home Secretary Roy Jenkins, included arrest without charge and deportation and exclusion without trial. The PTA, said Williams,

> is of course something that those of us in the labour movement, who have civil liberties very close to our hearts, cannot pretend to like. Of course we do not, and that is why its life has been put at six months — it will expire after six months — in the hope that it will not have to be extended.[12]

The Wilson government had secured the passage of the PTA through parliament without even a hint of a revolt from the Labour left. Williams' remarks suggested that the Labour national executive was also in agreement with the government's Irish policy. The Labour conference too failed to stage any substantial protest. None of this was surprising. The PTA calmed public opinion after 21 people died in a Birmingham pub bombing. Few politicians wished to risk the wrath of the electorate by making an issue of the PTA, even if it was a particularly savage attack on civil liberties. Moreover, the UWC strike had come as something of a shock to those in the Labour Party who were usually friendly to Ireland. The fall of Sunningdale had graphically illustrated that not all could be put right in the North of Ireland with a few strokes of a legislative pen. After Ulster's Protestants had ably demonstrated their intransigence, there were but two options for the British Labour government. One would have been to carry out Callaghan's threat to 'reconsider the link between Britain and North Ireland' and leave the Protestants to make out as they could in a united Ireland. The other was to copy their predecessors in the 1945-50 Labour government and give the Protestants what they wanted.

For a while it looked as though Wilson and Rees were moving in the direction of working for a united Ireland. Their path was paved more by expediency than conviction: the Birmingham carnage had not only produced the PTA. It had also sent the British government hurrying to the conference table to meet the Provisional IRA.

The talks began in January 1975 and were concluded a month later. One one side were British civil servants led by James Allen of the Foreign and Commonwealth Office. Facing them were two representatives of the Republican movement. The result was a military truce between Britain and the IRA. It began on 10 February.

Republican leader David O'Connell would later claim that the 'overall feature' of the truce, 'was a statement by the British government that it was committed to disengage from Ireland, but it could not say so publicly'. This withdrawal was to be 'planned and orderly... over a number of years'.[13]

The most substantial research into what happenéd at these negotiations has generally support O'Connell's version,[14] but the sincerity of what was promised is another matter. As with so many other aspects of the dealings between Labour governments and Ireland, these top secret talks were never reported to a full Cabinet meeting. From a British point of view, the best results of the talks was that it enabled the government to keep all options open.

The talks and the pressure from the IRA which precipitated

them did produce a result which internal critics of Labour policy had failed to achieve: internment was phased out by the end of 1975. By then, the truce had broken down over the Provisionals' insistence that Britain should make its policy public. Wilson's refusal to do so and the active sabotage of the truce by the Royal Ulster Constabulary brought this episode to a close. Merlyn Rees was moved to the Home Office in September.

The truce had a effect on inter-party relations at Westminster. For the first time, bipartisanship began to show signs of strain. The removal of Rees saw the inter-party fence-menders in action. Before the reshuffle, the Tory front bench had lobbied the name of Labour's Roy Mason to take over from Rees. A report in the *Irish Times* explained: 'The former Defence Secretary [Mason] is seen by opposition spokesmen on Northern Ireland as a politician prepared to adopt a tough security policy and defer more to British Army thinking'.[15] Tory support did not hurt Mason's chances and he was duly appointed.

September also saw Labour's NEC mulling over a proposed policy document on Northern Ireland. A document equally suited to be issued by the Tory party. It was written by Dick Barry, a member of the Labour Party's research staff, and, although it was rejected by the NEC, it undoubtedly represented a growing sentiment within the Labour Party. Barry was the party's chief research officer on Northern Ireland and his 'information paper' began by attacking the 'myths and legends which have grown up about the Irish question' and complained 'that there is considerable support within the labour movement for expelling the British army from Northern Ireland'.[16] The use of the verb 'expelling' dropped a heavy hint of what was to come — some of the most distorted, inaccurate material written on Ireland.

To say it was pro-Unionist is putting it mildly. Barry maintained:

> The Gladstonian argument in favour of granting Home Rule to Ireland was, basically that Ireland was a backward and foreign country which could not be governed democratically... the Liberals (and their Gladstonian Labour allies) were conscious of the fact that the Irish nationalist movement was socially reactionary.[17]

From this original interpretation of Gladstone's Irish

policy, Barry went on to assert: 'By 1906 the democratic revolution in Ireland was complete' and that 'the Irish nationalist or
"republican" movement was specifically... concerned to promote
the social power of the Roman Catholic Church'.[18] By contrast:
'After 1800 the Protestant community accepted the union and
the Protestant democrats got on with the job of pursuing their
class interests and seeking parliamentary reform with the United
Kingdom'.[19]

This re-write of history went on to reverse everything most
socialists in Britain and elsewhere had ever thought about
Ireland. James Connolly's Citizens' Army were said to be
'nationalist and class collaborationist'[20] so that the Protestants
in the North of Ireland from 1912-21, 'had no alternative but to
create a powerful political and military movement and to assert
their right to self-determination in opposition to Catholic
nationalism and British imperialism'.[21]

The virtues of Unionism after the Northern state was
established were also lauded by Barry. 'Anti-Catholic
discrimination was not a Unionist policy', he wrote. 'It arose in
response to Catholic nationalist attempts to disrupt democratic
government in Northern Ireland'.[22] Even the Loyalist terror
gangs of the early 1970s had been much misunderstood. Most
people had them down as sectarian killers. Labour's research
department now described them as 'counter-terrorist organisations'.[23]

Barry's document was Unionism with a vengeance. Its conclusion was based on its logic: 'Terrorism must be brought to an
end before there can be any reasonable prospect of further
political progress'.[24] Whether or not Roy Mason was influenced
by the document, it was to a military solution that he now turned.

Mason's tenure as Northern Ireland supremo from
September 1976 until the defeat of the Callaghan government in
May 1979 was the culmination of many preceding trends:
Labour's strengthening of partition in 1949; Wilson's early
neglect of the civil rights question; the use of British troops
'fighting on the side of Orange reactionaries' as Mellish had put
it. Above all else, 1976-79 saw the perfection of Labour/Tory
bipartisanship on Northern Ireland.

This was evident in the reception Mason's policies were
given by the Tory opposition, now under the leadership of

Margaret Thatcher. In December 1976, Airey Neave, Conservative spokesman on Northern Ireland, assured parliament that Mason 'had shown a determined and robust attitude to the security problems of Northern Ireland which the Opposition welcomes'.[25] In February 1977, Mason announced 'a further increase in the strength and effectiveness of the Ulster security forces'. Neave quickly 'welcomed' the changes and assured any doubters that 'what the government needed and Mr Mason was working on was a strategic plan to bring organised terrorism under control during 1977 and destroy the hopes of success of the IRA'.[26]

Although 'organised terrorism' was not brought 'under control' in 1977, this did not stop the Tories giving Mason top marks for effort. In September that year Tory MP John Biggs Davison told a meeting in his Epping Forest constituency that Mason was 'a champion of law and order'.[27] In November, Neave said that 'on the security front', Mason was 'putting into effect policies long advocated by the Conservative Party, such as the increased use of the Special Air Services (SAS)'.[28] The theme was repeated when Neave informed *Guardian* readers in May 1978 that Mason 'has already seemed anxious to adopt Conservative ideas on security and constitutional questions'.[29]

Why such blatant back-slapping for the parliamentary enemy? A clue is to be found in the Loyalists' attempt to organise a second general strike in May 1977. Mason dealt with the challenge with more firmness than Rees had during the UWC strike of 1974. Both the Army and RUC were more actively deployed this time. In fact the circumstances were different. Of all the Unionist and Loyalist politicians, only Ian Paisley of the far-right Democratic Unionist Party supported the strike. One of its aims was to bring back the old Stormont parliament, but that would have required a fundamental shift in British government policy. It would have amounted to handing over all authority to Paisley and his followers.

So Mason stood firm against Paisley and his demand for a transfer of power. Consequently the strike was defeated. Or was it? The strikers' second demand was for greater 'security' measures. To this Mason acquiesced. During the first days of the strike he had a meeting at the Ballylumford power station with Loyalist workers who were crucial to the outcome of the confrontation, since they controlled the production of most of the

North's electricity. To defeat Paisley, Mason had to win over these workers. After his meeting with them, and discussions with the Official Unionist leaders, Mason agreed to a number of 'security' proposals. The *Irish Times* reported:

> These included a build up of the RUC to a strength of 6,500 with more weapons, equipment and vehicles: an increase of the Ulster Defence Regiment's full-time strength to at least 1,800; a review of terrorist laws; increased emphasis of covert SAS-type activities and the formation of ten RUC divisional mobile support units.[30]

These proposals, which persuaded the power workers not to strike, did not come out of thin air. They were based on a long and detailed memorandum on security which had been presented to Mason by the Official Unionists.[31] Inter-party agreement on Northern Ireland now included consultation with the Unionists.

This was one consequence of the change in government emphasis — personified by Rees' replacement. As the *Sunday Times* put it: 'Callaghan sent Mason to Northern Ireland because he wanted a clear, unequivocal line to be taken, the priority being the defeat of terrorism, not further attempts to shuffle the well-thumbed politicial cards'.[32]

For a while it seemed as if the confident Mason just might pull it off. In February 1977, he said he was 'convinced that this message is getting through to the men of violence... they have set their feet on a road that goes nowhere'.[33] In October that year he asserted that the IRA 'has waned to the point where they cannot sustain a campaign'.[34] By the end of the year he was claiming that the 'tide has turned against the men of violence'.[35]

Eighteen months later a more realistic assessment was made by the British Army in Northern Ireland. In a top secret document, which found its way into the hands of the Provisionals, Army intelligence concluded:

> The Provisional IRA (PIRA) has the dedication and the sinews of war to raise violence intermittently to at least the level of early 1978, certainly for the forseeable future... PIRA will probably continue to recruit the men it needs. They will be able to attract enough people with leadership, talent, good education and manual skills to continue to enhance their all round professionalism. The movement will retain popular support sufficient to maintain secure bases in the traditional Republican areas.[36]

That was one verdict on the Labour government's get-tough policy. There were others, from such respected bodies as Amnesty International, the National Council for Civil Liberties and the Haldane Society of Socialist Lawyers.[37] The unanimity of their findings leaves no doubt that the Army and RUC killed innocent civilians, tortured 'confessions' from innocent men and women and harassed tens of thousands in Catholic working class ghettos.

What merits stressing is the responsibility of the Labour government for what happened in this period. It was not the case that a few soldiers or police lost their tempers. There were many examples of what the Amnesty Report called 'the maltreatment of suspected terrorists'. It is now known that as early as November 1977, before Amnesty had even begun its investigations, Labour's Attorney General Sam Silkin sent a confidential memorandum telling the Prime Minister of such goings-on.[38] This was the same Callaghan who had, in August 1969, toured the Catholic ghettos of Belfast and Derry promising civil rights and justice for all. Just eight years later, his premiership was turning large sections of the Catholic community to bitter hostility against everything British 'law and order' represented.

The ears of Callaghan and Mason were now deaf to those early demands for civil rights. The Special Powers Act had gone, only to be replaced by the Emergency Provisions Act and the Prevention of Terrorism Act. Despite Shirley Williams' 'hope' at the 1974 Labour Party conference, the latter did not expire after six months. It continued to be prolonged at regular intervals and was used to arrest such 'terrorists' as pacifist Pat Arrowsmith, Irish trade union leader Phil Flynn, Barry Silverman, prospective Labour candidate for Northwich, former Scotland Yard detective Arthur Evans and freelance journalist Ron McKay.[39]

Internment was phased out, but Northern Ireland Secretary Rees replaced it with a judicial process only marginally different. Those suspected of what the PTA defined as 'violence for political ends' were tried before a single judge without a jury, using rules of evidence often weighted in favour of the prosecution.[40]

The social and economic discrimination against Catholics also altered little during the ten years following the birth of the civil rights movement. In January 1978, the government's Fair

Employment Agency reported that Catholics in Northern
Ireland were two and a half times more likely to be unemployed
than Protestants, the report put it down to a question of skill:
'The model Protestant male is a skilled manual worker, whereas
the model Roman Catholic male is unskilled'.[41]

Such statistics did little to bear out Callaghan's assertion in
November 1978 that while Catholics 'were in a position of great
inferiority' in 1968, 'that's changed during the past decade'.[42].

For many Catholics all that had really changed were the
agents of their repression — British troops in the place of the
RUC and the 'B' Specials. As early as November 1976, Labour
MP Ian Mikardo had accused Mason of 'leaning too much
towards security',[43] and it was Mason's almost obsessional pursuit of military victories that led him to turn bitterly on anyone
or any institution he thought was standing in his way. In
November 1978 that while Catholics 'were in a position of great
outskirts of Belfast, Mason accused the BBC, in the presence of
its chairman, Northern Ireland controller and six directors, of
being disloyal, of 'trying to stir it' and of purveying the propaganda of the IRA. He claimed the IRA would have been
defeated 'years ago' had the government's Northern Ireland
Office been allowed to direct BBC policy. He ended by suggesting the BBC impose a 'three month blackout' on reporting
'terrorist activities'.[47]

In January 1978, he turned on Jack Lynch's Southern Irish
government, alleging it was responsible for the breakdown of
talks between the parties in Northern Ireland. In the same month
he hit out at critics of his policy from 'outside the UK' who had
'the effect of damaging confidence'.[45] Two months later Jack
Lynch was again the subject of Mason's belligerence. The Northern Ireland Secretary maintained that 'the bulk of terrorist
violence' emanated from Southern Ireland, and suggested that if
the Dail would co-operate the IRA would be defeated. The Irish
government was quick to retort that the figures supplied by the
British showed only two per cent of such violence had been
launched from the South. Mason stuck to his guns and received
high praise from one quarter. Enoch Powell, now Unionist MP
for South Down, told the House of Commons: 'The words which
fell from the Secretary of State this afternoon were the most impressive which have ever been used from the government front

bench on the subject'.[46]

In Mason's book, to even talk about Irish unity was now tantamount to sabotage. In April 1978, he told the Commons: 'Anybody who makes speeches about the unity of Ireland or national aspirations should bear in mind that it does make it much more politically difficult for me'.[47]

In November that year, he turned on the legal profession in Northern Ireland. They had been complaining about the physical state of suspects after police interrogation. Mason dismissed the protests as coming from 'those defence counsel who regularly defend IRA terrorists', a remark condemned by one MP as 'a slur on the legal profession'.[48]

But Mason's political prejudices were most apparent in February 1979 when he said in a radio interview that the Official Unionists were 'against sectarianism', and for 'bridging the political divide', while the Social Democratic Labour Party was become 'extreme'.[49] This was the last straw for the more moderate nationalist opinion. John Hume, deputy leader of the SDLP, called Mason 'anti-Irish',[50] while the *Irish Times* editorialised:

> The Secretary of State has finally written himself off as a serious, concerned arbiter of Northern Ireland politics... A British general election is approaching and Mr Mason may not be around for much longer. When he finally departs, he will leave behind the sorry record of a bankrupt approach to Irish politics.[51]

The antagonism of the SDLP and *Irish Times* towards Mason was not only based on his offhand radio remarks and the sorry civil liberties records of the Wilson/Callaghan governments. What angered most was the parliamentary pact between the Labour Party and the Official Unionists forged in July 1977. The deal also produced the most substantial revolt by Labour MPs against their party's Irish policy since 1949.

The cynical rationale of the alliance owed much to the prevailing parliamentary mathematics in the House of Commons. The Labour/Liberal parliamentary pact had come to an end; the government had lost a few by-elections; Labour no longer enjoyed a parliamentary majority; and the Scottish Nationalists had ended their support of Labour. Callaghan needed allies — or at least votes. He turned to the Official Unionists. In return for their support in parliament he offered to increase Northern Ireland's representation at Westminster, which would mean more seats for the Unionist majority.[52] At a press conference on 6 July, Official Unionist leader James Molyneaux announced his acceptance of the offer and promised his party would not vote against the government if its existence was at stake.

The Unionist demand for more seats in London was not a new one, but it had been repeatedly rejected by Labour's leaders. In August 1974, when the knife-edge Tory government was rumoured to be planning a similar pact with the Unionists, Harold Wilson told a television audience: 'It would be a grave dereliction of duty' if the Unionists were given more seats so that 'a future Conservative government' would 'get a few doubtful votes' at Westminster.[53] Four months before that Northern Ireland Secretary Rees had said:

> Many people in Northern Ireland, whatever we may think about it, look to the South and not this country... This is a fact of life... To talk of increased representation in this House in that context is not facing up to the facts of life... I do not see any circumstances in which extra representation of Northern Ireland, with its history, would be a means of bringing the peace we all want.[54]

Two years later Rees repeated the argument when he told the Commons: 'I visited many parts [of Northern Ireland] where even to talk about extra representation in this House is to fly in the face of history and cultural attitudes'.[55]

The flight against history and culture was now imminent. 'Illicit and sordid', Gerry Fitt, leader of the SDLP called it. He ended a Commons speech by declaring: 'No socialist with a drop of red blood in his veins could or should have allowed himself to be part of a deal to bring this Bill to this House'.[56] Fitt was attacking the Redistribution of Seats Bill, which gave Northern Ireland an extra six parliamentary seats, an increase of 50 per cent. His appeal to the socialist conscience of the Labour Party did not go unheard. Former Chief Whip Bob Mellish was the first to support Fitt in the Commons debate: 'I understand the manoeuvrings of government,' he said. 'I was part of them for years, but I would never stoop to that'.

It was, Mellish decided, time to rebel again:

I cannot vote for the Bill. I shall go into the lobby and vote against it. My principles and loyalties, not only to the Labour Party but to the people who are associated with me, will not allow me to support and perpetuate a system that was started in 1920, with the representation of the Ulster Unionists. I never wanted them, I do not want them now, and I live for the day when they are out of this House for ever.[57]

Kevin McNamara and Paul Rose were the other Labour MPs to voice their opposition in the debate. For Rose it was the last speech he was to make, 'before taking an agonising decision' to leave the Commons, and, 'remove myself from the masochistic pastime of knocking my head against the armour plating surrounding certain Ministers of the Crown'.[58]

Protests against the Bill were not confined to members who had campaigned on Ireland over the years. A total of 37 Labour MPs voted against their government. Two Parliamentary Private Secretaries, Ivor Clemitson and Bruce Grocott resigned their positions. They were joined by Jock Stallard, who quit his post as assistant Government Whip and told Callaghan in a letter that the Bill 'takes us away from a permanent, peaceful solution to our most serious domestic problem'.[59]

It had been the most substantial revolt the Callaghan government had had to face from its own benches. Subsequent events provided an ironic sequel that proved the rebellion entirely justified. As soon as the Unionists had achieved what they wanted — as well as the extra seats, they got the Labour government to prevent the extension of legalising adult homosexuality to Northern Ireland — they deserted Callaghan. The eventual upshot was a Tory motion of no confidence in the government. It was debated in parliament on 28 March 1979.

Callaghan needed the support of Gerry Fitt and Frank Maguire, the independent Republican MP for Fermanagh and South Tyrone, to survive. Both had always supported Labour in crucial votes. But not this time. Fitt told the Commons:

My grievances are very clear and readily understood. Although not too many of my honourable friends will say this in the House, many of them have told me that they recognise what has been going on over Northern Ireland and that they are heartily sorry. Many regret bitterly ever having done a deal with the devil in the person of the Northern Ireland Unionist Party. But it is too late now...

I have a loyalty to this government, to my own working class and trade union background, and to the whole working class movement in the United Kingdom and further afield. But I have a greater loyalty to the people of Northern Ireland. I am speaking with their voice tonight. It is their voice saying that because of what the government have done in the past five years — disregarded the minority and appeased the blackmailers of the Northern Ireland Unionist majority — I cannot go into the lobby with them tonight.[60]

And he didn't. Neither did Frank Maguire. The latter gave as his reason the refusal of the government to offer prison reforms to those in the H Blocks of Long Kesh. The Labour government fell by a majority of one: the immediate cause was its Irish policy. The chickens had finally come home to roost.

9. 'What about Ireland?'

SDLP leader Gerry Fitt, commenting further on his reasons for abstaining in the vote of no confidence in the Labour government in March 1979, remarked: 'When we look back in history, we see clearly that Labour governments are not the best governments to grapple with the Irish problem. That does not apply to Labour oppositions. When Labour is in opposition one sees the real conscience of the Labour Party'.[1]

The last time the Labour Party had been in opposition, from 1970-74, its actions had not suggested that Irish policy had a place in its 'real conscience'. Despite Wilson's advocacy of Irish unity within 15 years in 1972, bipartisanship saw out the end of the Heath government in 1974. It further flowered during Roy Mason's tenure at the Northern Ireland Office. Mason claimed in May 1979 that his term as Northern Ireland Secretary of State had made him 'internationally respected and admired'.[2] Some of Labour's leaders may not have shared all of that admiration, but there was little indication that any of them felt ready to display a fresh approach, now that they were in opposition.

Merlyn Rees, writing in the *Daily Express* on the tenth anniversary of British troops being despatched to Derry's Bogside, gave the ritualistic salute to the endeavours of the soldiers and declared: 'The United Kingdom government has the prime responsibility for Northern Ireland and it cannot be handed to anyone else. I would never be party to selling any group in Northern Ireland down any river, real or imaginary'.[3]

Michael Foot, speaking for the national executive at the 1979 Labour Party conference, defended bipartisanship and attacked a rather moderate resolution which called for 'consideration' of British presence in Ireland. Foot said the motion would lead to a 'complete misunderstanding' of Labour's policy.[4]

He and the NEC heavily criticised a resolution which called for an 'orderly withdrawal' of Britain from Ireland. Foot insisted: 'We must refuse to move in that direction at all'.[5]

In June 1980, Brynmor John, Labour's shadow spokesman on Northern Ireland, addressed the Gloucester Fabians and added his endorsement of bipartisanship as 'an agreement to share certain aims, namely the restoration of peace and a constitutional settlement to which both communities can adhere'. He criticised proposals that Labour should declare in favour of a united Ireland as having 'the effect of alienating one of the two communities',[6] although he don't appear to notice that not to do so alienated the other community.

Speeches on Ireland were few and far between during the 18 months following Labour's electoral defeat in May 1979. Brynmor John had said in his talk to the Fabians that 'to modern politicians Ireland is an unfashionable subject', a truism reflected by his own omission from the Shadow Cabinet. His appointment and that of his successor Don Concannon, as the party's Northern Ireland spokesmen illustrated the continuity of Labour's policy. John had been a defence ministry junior in the 1974 Wilson government, while Concannon as junior minister to Mason had been responsible for that administration's prisons policy. Both were on the right wing of the party. Neither nurtured the desire to challenge the by now institutionalised bipartisanship.

The lack of interest and radicalism towards Northern Ireland shown by Labour's leaders from May 1979, was nothing new. Until 1979 there had been no conference debate on the issue since 1974 — not that the party leadership was fighting tooth and nail to exclude such discussions; it did not have to since few constituency parties or trade unions had submitted resolutions. The apathy was also evident among the party's left wing. Their post mortems on the Wilson/Callaghan years virtually ignored Northern Ireland policy. In the two most important left critiques, Coates' *What Went Wrong*[7] and Tony Benn's *Arguments for Socialism*,[8] the word 'Ireland' did not appear.

A similar silence was to be found amongst important sections to the left of the Labour Party. Throughout the 1970s the Communist Party gave periodic endorsements to the Better Life For All Campaign, a list of aims drawn up by the Northern Ireland

Committee of the Irish Congress of Trade Unions. These included such worthy sentiments as the 'right to live free from violence' and the right to full employment, but avoided mentioning the national question which had been the over-riding issue in Irish politics for a decade. The irrelevancy of a Better Life For All was never more evident than in February 1978, when the Communist Party organised a London demonstration supporting it. An estimated 200 people attended.

Ireland had become a taboo subject even among influential marxists inside and outside the Labour Party. *New Left Review*, the most prominent marxist theoretical journal, carried not a single essay on Ireland during the 1970s.

There were exceptions to the wall of apathy. A number of trotskyist groups, notably the Internationabl Marxist Group (IMG), made Ireland one of their chief preoccupation in the 1970s. The IMG, the libertarian socialist group Big Flame, and, towards the end of the decade, the International Socialists — now the Socialist Workers' Party — put a lot of effort into building the Troops Out Movement (TOM) which in 1976 had replaced the Anti-Internment League. In the late 1970s TOM organised demonstrations in Britain that attracted several thousands. A few Labour Party members participated in TOM, but its actual membership never rose above several hundred.

The inability of TOM to build the 'mass campaign' it hoped for was due to the hostile environment it had to work in. The pro-Unionism of Britain's main political parties and the abstentionism which embraced the Labour left, the constituency activists and most of the marxists meant that Ireland remained a 'troublesome subject', in parliament or out of it.

The first signs of a challenge to the pro-Unionist, bipartisanship orthodoxy of Labour's leadership surfaced at the 1979 party conference.

Ten resolutions or amendments on Ireland were submitted. The majority came from constituencies in which there was a large Irish community, or where supporters of the Troops Out Movement had influence. The national executive and the conference arrangements committee were opposed to having a debate. Neil Kinnock, one of the more left wing members of the executive, offered the explanation that since the NEC didn't have a position on Ireland, the subject couldn't be debated![9]

A petition calling for a debate collected nearly 400
signatures and led to the conference voting two to one to discuss
the issue.

The debate lasted only half an hour and the composite
motions stressing immediate troop withdrawal and calling for an
end to bipartisanship were easily defeated, but the pressure produced an NEC promise to establish a sub-committee which would
look into formulating party policy on Ireland.

Those active on the issue of Ireland began to organise to
consolidate these small gains. In the spring of 1980, the Labour
Committee on Ireland was born at a London conference attended
by representatives from forty constituency Labour Parties. A
model resolution demanding that the next Labour government
'immediately begins the process of withdrawal' was one of 16
similar motions or amendments appearing on the 1980 party
conference agenda. The withdrawal demand was again easily
defeated, but more than half of the constituency party delegates
voted in favour. The NEC promised that the conclusions of the
1979 sub-committee study group would be ready by 1981.

MPs Jock Stallard, Joan Maynard and Ernie Roberts were
active in the Labour Committee on Ireland, but it was overwhelmingly composed of rank and file Labour Party members.
Some had been members of the Troops Out Movement, others
had been through one of the revolutionary socialist groups. The
Committee's twin demands for British withdrawal and an end to
bipartisanship still lacked the support of any influential member
of the Labour Party. A breakthrough came at the 1980 party
conference, at a fringe meeting organised by the LCI.

The main speaker was Tony Benn. Since the fall of the
Callaghan government he had emerged as the undisputed leader
of the Labour left and the champion of the constituency parties.
Benn began by referring to his father, William: 'I was brought
up to believe, very strongly, from my father that the partition of
Ireland was a crime', Tony Benn told his audience. 'My view has
never altered on that'.[10] He continued: 'I have never varied in my
view that there was no future for a policy based upon partition;
and no future for peace and co-operation in Ireland that did not
include a clear presentation of an alternative perspective of reunification and independence.'

Benn apologised for his previous silence on Ireland and went on to attack the lack of Cabinet discussion on the subject. He doubted whether trade union unity among Catholics and Protestants in Northern Ireland was possible in the short term and concluded: 'I believe that the presence and the continued presence of the British as a political and military force in Northern Ireland is the major barrier that stands in the way of trade union and Labour Party unity. The sooner we withdraw the better.'

Benn's public association with the cause of British withdrawal was a substantial gain for the Labour Committee on Ireland. He had a profound influence on many rank and file members of the Labour Party; equally important, his remarks encouraged some of his more important advisers to include the record of the previous Labour government's policy on Ireland within the general critique they were making of the Wilson/Callaghan years. Chris Mullin, deputy editor of *Tribune*, launched a fierce attack on Mason's policy in the pamphlet *How to Reselect Your MP* which was published by the Campaign for Labour Party Democracy and the Institute for Workers' Control in early 1981. Mullin advised constituency parties to check whether their MP had voted against the Prevention of Terrorism Act and the Emergency Provisions Act before supporting reselection.

Members of the Bennite left were not alone in demanding change. A backbench group of Labour MPs, organised in the Northern Ireland Parliamentary Group, was also on the offensive. They included traditional campaigners like Jock Stallard and Kevin McNamara, former government Ministers Patrick Duffy and Reg Freeson, as well as some of the newer MPs like Clive Soley, Alf Dubbs and Joan Maynard, who was also on Labour's NEC.

The Northern Ireland Parliamentary Group, which was the successor to the Campaign for Democracy in Ulster, had been established in the early 1970s, but only began functioning regularly after the fall of the Callaghan government. It made its priority the NEC study group, submitting a 3,500-word paper entitled *Northern Ireland — Some Options for an All-Ireland Solution*[11] in the autumn of 1980. Written by Reg Freeson, it had received the general endorsement of the group, which by that time had 32 members.

The paper highlighted the widening gulf between the Northern Ireland Parliamentary Group and the parliamentary leadership. Not all of the group were on the left wing of the party — some represented constituencies holding significant Irish communities. They were a hetrogeneous collection of individuals united only by an interest in finding a solution to the Northern Ireland stalemate. This led them to conclude in the Freeson paper: 'Britain's objectives in Ulster should be withdrawal of troops to barracks as soon as possible, social and economic reform, reconciliation and the peaceful reunification of Ireland.'

The report went on to give a short, but informative and balanced history of Ireland, Britain's divisive role over the years and the Labour Party's past attitudes on both. Freeson noted the policy of the December 1920 special Labour Party conference and observed: 'Irish questions, in fact, never again were an important part of thinking within the British Labour Party and movements until events in the late '60s and '70s forced them to become so.'

Calling for 'open political discussion' Freeson insisted: 'I want that discussion now and if bipartisanship stands in the way, then bipartisanship should go'. As to the direction of this discussion, his paper called for 'the withdrawal of the army from Northern Ireland — a planned, orderly and progressive withdrawal, provided the police is organised to involve Catholic and Protestant communities; and provided it is accompanied by a political initiative which includes the prospect of a united Ireland.'

He outlined a series of proposals to accompany this 'planned, constructive disengagement from Northern Ireland'. These included safeguards for the Protestant minority in a united Ireland, interim power-sharing in the North and a timetable for British withdrawal. While not explicitly stated in the paper, the inference was that Britain should get out and Ireland be unified whether or not the Northern majority agreed.

Freeson's paper broke with the three basic tenets which had informed Labour policy on Ireland since Herbert Morrison's meeting with Basil Brooke in 1946: support for partition, bipartisanship at Westminster and backing for the right of the Unionists in Northern Ireland to veto any constitutional change.

By now, it was obvious that British policy in Ireland had been unsuccessful. The failure of one political initiative after another, the continued resilience of the Provisionals, the rise of Ian Paisley to the leadership of the Protestant community — illustrated by his topping the poll in Northern Ireland in the 1979 election for the European Parliament — all exposed the bankruptcy of Westminster policy on Ireland.

Some notable military successes for the IRA, particularly the assassination of the Queen's uncle Lord Mountbatten and the killing of 19 soldiers at Warrenpoint on the same day on 26 August 1979, added to the British feeling that something had to be done. In the Labour Party, war-weariness was compounded by the general left wing drift within the party, particularly at constituency level. On top of all this, public opinion was becoming more and more disenchanted with the whole Irish business, as opinion polls showed and had been hinted as early as August 1979 when the *Daily Mirror*, Fleet Street's traditional Labour supporter, called for Britain to declare its intent to leave Ireland within five years.[12]

Not until the very end of its deliberations did the study group which had been announced by Callaghan at the 1979 party conference take into consideration this tide of opinion. When it was set up, membership of the study group was evenly balanced between pro- and anti-partitionists.

But the former were assisted by having as secretary of the group Dick Barry, author of the fervent pro-Unionist research paper of 1976. He was supposed to share the secretaryship with David Lowe, who researched internationally matters for the Labour Party and was sympathetic to the concept of a united Ireland. In practice, Lowe was edged out. In July 1980, Lowe wrote to the group chairman Alex Kitson to complain of being deliberately excluded from a delegation visiting Southern Ireland.

The majority of those the study group met on this and other visits to Ireland were Unionist. On a visit to Northern Ireland from 27-30 June 1980, members of the study group met the Official Unionist Party, the Progressive Unionist Party, the Democratic Unionist Party, the Northern Ireland Labour Party, the Alliance Party, the New Ulster Political Research Group, the United Labour Party and the Campaign for Labour Representation. All of these organisations were in differing degree pro-partition. Some, particularly the Campaign for Labour Representation and the United Labour Party had very few members. What they did have was the explicit 'two nations' view of Irish politics endorsed by Dick Barry.

The study group delegation also met the Republican Clubs and the Labour and Trade Union Group. The former was the Northern wing of Sinn Fein, the Workers' Party, formerly the Official Sinn Fein. Despite their name, the Republican Clubs had swung over to a pro-partition position by calling for the return of the Northern Ireland parliament which the Tories had dissolved in 1972. As for the Labour and Trade Union Group, it shared many of the views advocated by the *Militant* newspaper, particularly the call for a new Labour Party in Northern Ireland.

The only Northern Ireland political organisation the study group met which was anti-partitionist was the Social and Democratic and Labour Party.[13]

When they visited Southern Ireland they met the three main political parties, all of whom were anti-partitionist, at least in theory. They also talked to Socialists Against Nationalism, another small 'two nations' organisation. But neither in the North nor the South of Ireland did the group meet Provisional Sinn Fein, which, in terms of number of councillors was the fourth largest party in the South. No other republican or nationalist political organisation met the study group.

Considering the selective nature of its choice when collecting its evidence, the first public statement of the study group contained no surprises. *Northern Ireland: The Next Steps?*[14] contained a short, five paragraph historical introduction, followed by the posing of five questions. It was drafted by Dick Barry.

The content of *The Next Steps?* was summarised by Kevin McNamara in a speech to Formbay and Altcar Labour Party in March 1981. He reflected the hostility with which the document was received by significant sections of the Labour Party.[15]

McNamara began by calling *The Next Steps?*

A dangerous, foolish paper, a Unionist paper, some might be a little unkind to call it an Orange paper... It bases itself on the continuing assumption of the Six Counties being part and remaining a definite part of the United Kingdom. The whole drift of its argument is in favour of integration of the Six

Counties within the United Kingdom.

The first part of the document dealt with the Northern Ireland economy. The study group suggested closer ties between Britain and Northern Ireland, suggesting the construction of a gas pipeline across the Irish Sea. Instead, McNamara called for the economic integration of Ireland, with a gas pipeline running from the Kinsale field in the South to Belfast.

The second part concerned civil rights. In his reply McNamara suggested discrimination in Ulster was an intrinsic part of the Northern state. He again placed the issue in an all-Ireland context, suggesting the South change some of the laws which Northern Unionists felt reflected a purely Catholic morality.

In his response to that part of the document that dealt with forms of government, McNamara bitterly attacked its 'Orange flavour', noting its calls for either the return of a non-power sharing Northern Ireland parliament, or complete integration of Northern Ireland with Britain. McNamara argued simply for unification and British withdrawal, 'because I do not believe that Britain should be there'.

Part four of the document tackled whether the Labour Party should extend its organisation to Northern Ireland, or help to establish a new party in the province. McNamara criticised both options for their partitionist assumptions.

Finally there was the question of 'security'. McNamara called for the scrapping of the PTA and the Emergency Provisions Act.

He ended his speech by calling for a complete rejection of the study group paper: 'Let us start with the concept of the island of Ireland and work from that, rather than looking at the Six Counties as some sort of imperial relic'.

McNamara had not gone out on a limb simply to voice his own convictions. He told his audience he was expressing and expanding the views that members of the Northern Ireland Parliamentary Group had made to the study group.

A deep and public breach was now opening between a powerful backbench committee of Labour MPs and the party's national executive, which had endorsed the study group's paper. This gulf went largely unobserved at the time — given that differences of opinion between the PLP and the NEC were nothing new. What distinguished the breach on this issue was that the PLP group were to the left of the NEC. It was the PLP group which was putting forward a traditional socialist policy; it was the NEC which was cautious and conservative.

Amongst the rank and file the views McNamara was promoting were gaining greater acceptance. The NEC gave the constituency parties just over two months to formulate and submit their opinions, a limited opportunity considering the slow-moving nature of the CLPs. Yet the study group received 79 responses. Of the 67 from Britain, 48 came from local Labour Parties.[16] The internal assessment of this evidence was forced to conclude: 'The only clear cut pattern which emerges from the evidence favours the concepts of a united Ireland, opposes the organisation of the Labour Party in Northern Ireland, and calls for the withdrawal of troops'.[17]

Such views had little initial influence on the majority of the study group. At the end of February, one member, Don Concannon, was still arguing strongly against any concessions to a united Ireland.[18] At the end of March, secretary Barry and chairman Kitson overturned an earlier decision of the study group made in their absence that the Labour Party should not organise in Northern Ireland.[19]

Then, on 10 April 1981 a by-election in the Northern Ireland constituency of Fermanagh and South Tyrone upset many calculations, not least those of the Labour Party's NEC study group.

The poll was caused by the death of Frank Maguire, the MP whose abstention in the crucial vote of no confidence had helped bring down the Labour government.

Maguire's reason for his refusal to save Callaghan's skin had been the Northern Ireland prisons policy of the Labour government. Since March 1976 Republican prisoners in the H Blocks of Long Kesh — officially 'The Maze' — had been involved in various protests to try to win back the political 'special category status' they had won from the Tory administration in 1972, but which had been abolished by Merlyn Rees four years later. The prisoners argued that as they had been arrested, interrogated and tried under special legislation, they merited different prison treatment from that of 'ordinary criminals'. In short, they demanded to be treated as prisoners-of-war. Neither the Callaghan nor Thatcher government budged on the issue. In

October 1980, a group of prisoners went on hunger strike, attracting mass sympathy in Ireland, but evoking little response elsewhere. The strike ended a few days before Christmas, with the prisoners claiming the Northern Ireland Office had promised a number of concessions. When these were not forthcoming the hunger strike began again on the 1 March 1981. This time it was started by a single prisoner, Bobby Sands.

For a fortnight the young republican's strike appeared to be attracting less support in Ireland than the previous one. Frank Maguire's death began a chain of events which changed that dramatically. Bobby Sands stood in the by-election for Maguire's seat. In a straight fight with the Official Unionist, Harry West, he won — polling more than 30,000 votes.

Sands, now MP, continued to starve in prison and on 5 May he died. When his death was announced to the House of Commons, Thatcher repeated her government's determination to make no concessions to the prisoners, including those who had followed Sands on hunger strike. Bipartisanship was still the order of the day. As *The Times* reported: 'There were loud cheers from all parts of the Commons yesterday as Mr Michael Foot, leader of the Labour Party, placed himself squarely behind Mrs Margaret Thatcher in her firm rejection of the demands of the IRA hunger strikers'.[20]

The one discordant note came from Patrick Duffy, a junior Defence Minister in the Callaghan government and member of the PLP Northern Ireland Group. He attacked Foot's 'metooism' as well as the 'intransigence' of Thatcher, accusing the government of 'moral bankruptcy' and 'criminal incompetence'.

Duffy's was not the first protest of Labour MPs over the government's handling of the hunger strike. At the beginning of 14 May, Labour backbenchers, mainly on the left of the party, had called for 'a serious move by the government to end the crisis'.[21] Tony Benn had urged the shadow Cabinet and the *Tribune* group to campaign for Sands to take his seat at Westminster; his advice was rejected. On 3 May, left wing MP Martin Flannery had attacked a visit Don Concannon had paid to Sands, a few days before the latter's death. Concannon told the dying MP he would receive no support from the Labour Party, an action described by Flannery as 'unimaginative, totally insensitive and like sending a British tank to a Northern Ireland funeral'.[22]

But it was Patrick Duffy's remarks which suggested the Labour opposition leadership was now facing something more substantial than criticisms from left wing MPs. Duffy was firmly entrenched in the centre of the party and his anger encouraged others.

In a radio interview a week after Sands' death, Tony Benn called for the withdrawal of British troops, and their replacement by a United Nations force. 'The British government,' said Benn, 'has no long-term future in Ireland'.[23] Benn's statement was made in the context of his fight for the deputy leadership of the Labour Party. Accordingly, Ireland became an issue in the contest. One of Benn's campaign organisers, Peter Hain, used an article in the *Guardian* on 18 May to call for British withdrawal and a united Ireland.

Even some members of the right wing of the Labour Party were forced to back pedal. Merlyn Rees told a TV interviewer on 17 May that the removal of the right of the majority in Northern Ireland to veto any constitutional change might be 'a good step'.[24] More dramatically, the former party leader and Prime Minister James Callaghan was now calling for British withdrawal and an independent Northern Ireland. 'Does anyone really believe,' he asked,

> that our dual policy of direct rule combined with firmness will result in Northern Ireland emerging permanently — I utter the word permanently — from years of torment, with its people reconciled to the existing relationship with Britain? I must answer the question in the negative.[25]

The new mood was not confined to the PLP. Constituency parties submitted more than sixty resolutions or amendments on Ireland to Labour's 1981 conference. The majority called for British withdrawal, an end to bipartisanship and a united Ireland. The pressure was too great for the NEC study group to resist. Its final report, issued on the eve of conference, set out the objective of 'unity between the two parts of Ireland'.[27] The study group sought to tone this objective down by insisting that any change in Northern Ireland's constitutional position would have to be approved by a referendum, but this proviso was thrown out by the NEC.

Why this turnaround? Why was the study group obliged to change its conclusion? Why did Rees and Callaghan break with their own history? Why did the Bennite left adopt Ireland as a major issue? Why did so many CLPs add their names to the cause of British withdrawal?

There were a number of reasons. Benn's previous statements on Ireland; the work of the Labour Committee on Ireland; the work of the PLP back-bench group; the continuing impasse of British policy in Ireland. But the spark that lit the fire was the parliamentary election of Bobby Sands. Joan Maynard told an LCI fringe meeting at the 1981 party conference: 'Bobby Sands' death and the votes he got transformed the situation inside the Parliamentary Labour Party. As far as Irish unity went, it was mass conversions all round'.[27] The Sands victory has also awakened world-wide interest in Northern Ireland. This interest was overwhelmingly hostile to Britain,[28] and gave Labour further cause for reflection.

The culminative effect on Labour MPs was shown when the Representation of the People Bill was brought before Parliament. Its purpose was to prevent a repetition of the Sands victory by prohibiting prisoners from standing in elections. Labour opposed the Bill when it was given a second reading on 22 August. Their home affairs spokesman, Roy Hattersley, defended 'the right of a constituency to elect an MP of its choice',[29] and George Cunningham, another member of the home affairs team, complained: 'MPs constantly told the IRA to make use of the ballot box. It could not be denied that in Fermanagh the ballot box was made use of. It did not make sense to change the law'.[30] The Labour leadership allowed a free vote on the measure and 137 MPs, the vast majority Labour, voted against. The Bill was carried with a majority of 111.

The rare occurrence of a breakdown in bipartisanship was not hard to explain. Throughout its history, the Labour Party had insisted on the use of the ballot box to change society — indeed, it was on this perspective the party had been established. If the same opportunity was to be denied to others, then Labour's own political ideology was under threat. The attitude of much of the party to the Representation of the People Bill in 1981 was not dissimilar to the warning voiced by V. Hartshorn, a Labour MP, in 1919, when he said that 'parliamentary institutions' were 'on trial' and that the government's refusal to acknowledge Sinn Fein's election victory in Ireland could lead to 'the conclusion that parliamentary government is fraud'.

There is a further parallel between 1918-20 and 1981. The 1918 Sinn Fein poll victory forced the Labour Party to try to formulate its own Irish policy. The Sands' victory, followed by the election of his agent Owen Carron in the same constituency and the success of two more Northern Irish prisoners in winning seats in the Southern Ireland parliament, produced a similar pressure.

One other comparison can be made. From 1918 to 1920, the views of Irish trade unionists were sought and, to some extent, adhered to by the British Labour Party. In June 1981, a group of leading Irish trade unionists, mainly based in the South, tried the same tack. They wrote to Ron Hayward, general secretary of the Labour Party, calling for an end to both bipartisanship and the Unionists' right to veto, urging instead 'a policy of working constructively towards Irish reunification'.[31] Signatures included eight trade union general secretaries who claimed they were expressing 'the majority view of Irish trade unionists on the Northern Ireland problem.'

The second 1920 conference of the Labour Party had heeded the views of Irish trade unionists. The majority at the 1981 conference did not. Two resolutions calling for British withdrawal from Ireland, support for Irish unity and an end to the Unionist veto were defeated. However, the vast majority of constituency delegates did support a milder withdrawal motion. The PLP Northern Ireland groups adopted a similar position. The conference as a whole preferred to accept the study group's report amended by the NEC.

The conference reflected the gains the Irish oppositionists had made over six months. Irish unity now became the long-term objective of the Labour Party. There was a commitment to repeal the Prevention of Terrorism Act and to 'review' the Emergency Provisions Act.

In other areas the pro-Unionists won out. The NEC report endorsed a call for a labour movement conference in Northern Ireland to discuss the possibility of forming a six-county Labour Party, although this proposal had been supported by only four of the 68 submissions made to the study group.[32] The report also maintained 'the right of the Northern Ireland people to remain within the UK' and made clear that 'it would be no part of the political programme of the Labour Party to force Northern Ireland out of the United Kingdom'.[33]

Thereby, if the 1981 conference defeated moves towards unqualified all-Irish self-determination, while the reverse had occurred at the first 1920 conference. The Irish unity policy agreed at the 1981 conference was more vague than the 15-point programme put forward by Harold Wilson in 1972.

Eighty-two years into the twentieth century, the British Labour Party had still to resolve the conflict between three of its traditional commitments when it came to applying them to Ireland.

The first is a commitment to the principle and practice of majority rule. Support for this, as regards Ireland, was expressed by the Social Democratic Federation, the Councils of Action in 1920, the first 1920 party conference, the Ireland Act rebels of 1949 and the Labour Committee on Ireland and others in 1981. The second commitment is to the promotion of reforms through and by British parliamentary institutions. In the Irish context, this was made a priority by Labour supporters of the early Home Rule movement, by Michael Foot in 1949, when he filled the columns of the *Daily Herald* with support for the Northern Irish state but suggested internal improvement, and by the half-hearted attempts of the Labour governments of 1968-70 and 1974-76 to bring 'civil rights' to the people of Northern Ireland.

The third commitment — to see to all such matters as subservient to the interests of the British state — has been well maintained. It was reflected in the limitations placed on Irish self-determination by the party's leaders in the first two decades of the twentieth century, by the Labour Cabinet of 1949 and by the Callaghan/Mason regime of 1976-79.

The Labour Party has often tried to bring together these three commitments — this has always resulted in compromise, consensus and fudging. The Irish national question has proved itself resistant to resolution by such means.

The Labour Party has always been the party of the middle way. But there is little evidence that there is a navigable middle way in Ireland, or that there ever has been. Unfortunately, there is much evidence to suggest that too many in Britain, including the Labour Party, refuse to recognise this.

The Irish national question continues to inch towards a progressive conclusion. What role the British Labour Party will play in the progress has yet to be determined. But only a J.H. Thomas, Herbert Morrison or Roy Mason would have the audacity to defend much of its past behaviour. The attitudes and relationships of the British Labour Party to Ireland have been neither honourable, internationalist, nor socialist. The use of the last adjective may raise definitional controversies, but the question thrown at Labour MP, James O'Grady, by members of the Russian soviets more than sixty years ago lies on the table: 'What about Ireland, what about Ireland?'

Until the British Labour Party can come up with better answers than defending the division of Ireland and its working class, than headshaking over dead hunger strikers and handshaking with its Tory opponents, then Labour's definition of socialism will remain the most curious of all.

References

1. The Inheritance pages 1-15

1. T.W. Moody, 'Michael Davitt and the British Labour Movement', in *Transactions of the Royal Historical Society*, fifth series, volume 3 1953, p.57.
2. *ibid*. p.63
3. Henry Pelling, *Origins of the Labour Party*, Oxford: Clarendon Press 1965, p.43.
4. *Radical*, 1 April 1981.
5. Walter Kendall, *The Revolutionary Movement in Britain*, Weidenfeld and Nicolson, London: 1969, p.4.
6. Pelling, *op.cit*. p.18.
7. Moody, *op.cit*. p.62.
8. Yvonne Kapp, *Eleanor Marx: The Crowded Years*, London: Virago 1979, p.198.
9. H.M. Hyndman, *Further Reminiscences*, London: Macmillan 1912, p.56.
10. Kapp, *op.cit*. pp.198-9.
11. Marx and Engels, *Selected Correspondence*, Moscow: Foreign Languages Publishing House 1965, p.237.
12. *ibid*. p.230.
13. *ibid*. pp.236-7.
14. See for example Tom Nairn, 'Anatomy of the Labour Party', in Robin Blackburn, *Revolution and Class Struggle*, London: Fontana 1977.
15. Ian Cummings, *Marx, Engels and National Movements*, London: Croom Helm 1980, p.106.
16. *ibid*. p.109.
17. Moody, *op.cit*. p.57.
18. Independent Labour Party (ILP) Conference Report 1899, p.13.
19. A. McBriar, *Fabian Socialism and English Politics*, Cambridge: Cambridge University Press 1962, p.119.
20. Marx and Engels, *op.cit*. pp.411-12.
21. Stanley Pierson, *British Socialists*, London: Harvard University Press 1979, p.41.
22. Moodie, *op.cit*. p.71.

23. *Local Government in Ireland*, Fabian Tract 99, London: Fabian Society 1900, p.2.
24. *ibid*. p.13.
25. Samuel Levenson, *James Connolly*, London: Martin, Brian and O'Keeffe 1973, p.68.
26. *ibid*. p.66.
27. *ibid*. p.56.
28. Marx and Engels, *op.cit*. p.453.
29. These and the following election addresses are in the Labour Party archives.
30. *ILP Conference Report*, 1901, p.29.
31. Ralph Miliband, *Parliamentary Socialism*, London: Merlin Press 1972, p.17.
32 Henry Pelling, *A Short History of the Labour Party*, London: Macmillan 1961, p.29.
33. Pelling, *Origins of the Labour Party*, p.59.
34. *ILP Conference Report*, 1901, p.40.
35. Kapp *op.cit*. p.735.
36. Pelling, *Origins of the Labour Party*, p.58.
37. Miliband, *op.cit*. p.115.
38. Michael Davitt, *The Fall of Feudalism in Ireland*, London: 1903, p.377.
39. Keir Hardie, *Speeches and Writings*, Glasgow: 1915, p.38.
40. Fred Reid, *Keir Hardie: The Making of a Socialist*, London: Croom Helm 1979, p.115.
41. Moodie, *op.cit*. p.67.
42. *ibid*. p.72.
43. *ibid*. p.72.
44. *ibid*. p.74.
45. Marx and Engels, *op.cit*. p.351.

2. 'A. Detached Party' pages 16-33

1. *Labour Representation Committee, Conference Report*, 1901, p.20.
2. Labour Party archives, LRC 25/258.
3. *ibid*. LRC 26/25.
4. *ibid*. LRC 26/34.
5. *ibid*. LRC 26/35.
6. Geoffrey Bell, *The Protestants of Ulster*, London: Pluto Press 1976, pp.73-4.
7. Labour Party archives, LRC 25/318.
8. *ibid*. LRC 25/519.

9. *ibid*. LRC executive, 9/10/1905.

10. Emanuel Shinwell, *I've Lived Through It All*, London: Gollancz 1973, p.53.

11. Labour Party archives, LRC 25/190.

12. Miliband, *op.cit*. p.28.

13. *Labour Party Conference Report*, 1907, p.3.

14. *ibid*. p.43.

15. J.D. Clarkson, *Labour and Nationalism in Ireland*, New York: 1925, p.206.

16. See Bell, *op.cit*. pp.72-4 and *The Connolly/Walker Controversy*, Cork: Cork Workers' Club 1974.

17. Clarkson, *op.cit*. p.255.

18. *Independent Labour Party Conference Report*, 1908, pp.41-2.

19. *Labour Party Conference Report*, 1910, p.55.

20. Parliamentary Debates (Hansard), House of Commons 1912 Vol.34, cols.481-2.

21. *Labour Party Conference Report*, 1913, p.38.

22. *ibid*. p.71.

23. Clarkson, *op.cit*. p.465.

24. Charles McCarthy, *Trade Unionism in Ireland 1894-1960*, Dublin: 1977, p.43.

25. See for example Emmett Larkin, *James Larkin, Irish Labour Leader, 1876-1947*, New American Library, Mentor, 1968.

26. *ibid*. p.132.

27. *ibid*. p.132.

28. Levenson, *op.cit*. p.242.

29. *Daily News*, 22 September 1913.

30. *Leicester Pioneer*, 6 October 1913.

31. Larkin, *op.cit*. p.134.

32. Labour Party archives, LP/DUB/13/22-92.

33. Bob Holton, *British Syndicalism*, London: Pluto Press 1976, p.194.

34. George Dangerfield, *The Damnable Question*, London: Quartet 1979, p.62.

35. *ibid*. p.71.

36. F.S.L. Lyons, *Ireland Since the Famine*, London: Fontana 1973, p.303.

37. *ibid*. p.302.

38. Hansard, 1913 Vol.53, col.1493.

39. *ibid*. Vol.53, col. 1497.

40. Henry Patterson, *Class Conflict and Sectarianism*, Belfast: Blackstaff Press 1940, p.83.

41. Bell, *op.cit*.

42. Hansard, 1913 Vol.53, col.1497.

43. Lyons, *op.cit.* p.303.
44. Hansard, 1914 Vol.59, col.938-9.
45. *ibid.* 1914 Vol.60, col.145.
46. P. Beresford Ellis (ed.), *James Connolly, Selected Writings*, London: Penguin 1973, p.275.
47. *Forward*, 25 September 1920.
48. Levenson, *op.cit.* p.324.
49. *Morning Post*, 14 May 1916.
50. P. Beresford Ellis, *A History of the Irish Working Class*, London: Gollancz 1972, p.232.
51. *Labour Party Conference Report*, 1917, p.42.

3. The Search for a Policy   pages 34-46

1. Beresford Ellis, *A History of the Irish Working Class*, p.231.
2. Hansard, 1916 Vol.86, cols.626-7.
3. Dangerfield, *op.cit.* p.254.
4. *Labour Party Conference Report*, 1917, p.42.
5. Hansard, 1916 Vol.84, col.629.
6. *ibid.* 1917 Vol.98, cols.734-5.
7. Pelling, *A Short History of the Labour Party*, p.42.
8. Dangerfield, *op.cit.* p.269.
9. *ibid.* p.272.
10. *Labour Party Conference Rèport*, 1918, p.16.
11. *ibid.* p.69.
12. Hansard, 1918 Vol.109, col.181.
13. *Labour Party Conference Report*, 1919, p.185.
14. Hansard, 1918 Vol.112, col.143.
15. *ibid.* cols.158-9.
16. *Labour Party Conference Report*, 1919, p.185.
17. *Labour Party Conference Report*, 1920, p.6.
18. Hansard, 1919 Vol.114, cols.1502-3.
19. *ibid.* cols.1506-7.
20. Hansard, 1919 Vol.115, cols. 1697-8.
21. Miliband, *op.cit.* p.72.
22. Hansard, 1919 Vol.115, col.1709.
23. Dangerfield, *op.cit.* p.314.

4. The Policy Challenged   pages 47-68

1. Hansard, 1920 Vol.127, col.948.
2. *ibid.* cols.95-2.
3. *ibid.* col.957.
4. *Daily Herald*, 26 February 1920.

5. *Forward*, 3 April 1920.
6. *Labour Party Conference Report*, 1920, p.6.
7. Clarkson, *op.cit.* p.413.
8. *ibid.* pp.413-14.
9. Hansard, 1920 Vol.129, col.1328.
10. *ibid.* col.1344.
11. *ibid.* col.1350.
12. George Bernard Shaw, *Irish Nationalism and Labour Internationalism*, London: Labour Party 1914, p.5.
13. *ibid.* p.10.
14. *ibid.* p.13.
15. Raymond Challinor, *The Origins of British Bolshevism*, London: Croom Helm 1977, p.267.
16. *Forward*, 17 May 1920.
17. *ibid.*
18. *Labour Party Conference Agenda,* 1920, p.21.
19. *Labour Party Conference Report*, 1920, p.161.
20. *ibid.* p.160.
21. *ibid.* p.161.
22. *ibid.* p.164.
23. *ibid.* p.166.
24. *ibid.* p.166.
25. Miliband, *op.cit.* p.28.
26. *Labour Party Conference Report*, 1920, p.167.
27. Clarkson, *op.cit.* p.421.
28. *ibid.*
29. Labour Party archives, CA/gen/595.
30. *ibid.* CA/gen/607.
31. *ibid.* CA/gen/740.
32. *ibid.* CA/gen/886.
33. *ibid.* CA/gen/615.
34. *ibid.* CA/gen/815.
35. *ibid.* CA/gen/741, and many similar in CA/gen file.
36. *ibid.* CA/gen/755.
37. *ibid.* CA/gen/756.
38. *ibid.* CA/gen/1013.
39. *ibid.* CA/gen/543.
40. *ibid.* CA/gen/74.
41. Nan Milton, *John Maclean,* London: Pluto Press 1973, p.238.
42. *Labour Party Conference Report*, 1921, p.73.
43. Labour Party archives, EC minutes, 18 October 1920.
44. Hansard, 1920 Vol.134, cols.1416-17.
45. Hansard, 1920 Vol.138, col.629.
46. *Labour Party Conference Report*, 1921, p.23.

47. Labour Party archives, EC minutes, 28 December 1921. Report of the Labour Commission to Ireland, Labour Party, 1921, p.118.
49. D.G. Boyce, *Englishmen and Irish Troubles*, London: Jonathan Cape 1972, pp.62-3.
50. *The Times*, 18 February 1921.
51. Boyce, *op. cit.* pp.70-71.
52. Labour Party Conference Agenda, 1921, p.26.
53. Hansard, 1921 Vol.147, cols.1407-8.
54. Dangerfield, *op.cit.* p.341.
55. Hansard, 1921 Vol.149, cols.18-22.
56. *ibid.* col.311.

5. Making Partition Concrete   pages 69-85

1. *The Times*, 31 August 1920.
2. *Socialist Challenge*, 10 December 1980.
3. Public Record Office, CAB 23/48.
4. *ibid.*
5. Other payments were also involved. See Lyons, *op.cit.* pp.610-14.
6. Hansard, 1932 Vol.265, col.184.
7. *ibid.* col.1282.
8. *ibid.*
9. Hansard, 1932 Vol.268, col.544.
10. G. Blaxland, *J.H. Thomas: A Life for Unity*, London: Muller 1964, p.262.
11. *Labour Party Conference Report*, 1926, p.245.
12. Denis Gwynn, *The History of Partition*, Dublin: Browne and Nolan 1950, p.224.
13. Hansard, 1935 Vol.304, col.1384-5.
14. Farrell, *op.cit.* pp.141-2.
15. F. McManus, *The Years of the Great Test 1926-39*, Dublin: Mercier 1967, p.147.
16. Hansard, 1939 Vol.350, col.1102.
17. *Labour Party Conference Report*, 1945, p.108.
18. Bernard Donoughue and G.W. Jones, *Herbert Morrison*, London: Weidenfeld and Nicolson 1973, pp.307-8.
19. Public Record Office (PRO), CAB/21/13.
20. Farrell, *op.cit.* p.40.
21. *ibid.* p.95.
22. Bell, *op.cit.* p.40.
23. Donoughue and Jones, *op.cit.* p.307.
24. PRO CAB/21/13.
25. PRO CAB/129/13.

26. PRO CAB/21/13.
27. PRO CAB/128/6.
28. PRO CAB/128/13.
29. *ibid.*
30. PRO CAB/129/31.
31. Douglas Savoy, *Contemporary History of Ireland*, Belfast: Ulster Unionist Council 1958, p.41.
32. Hansard, 1949 Vol.464, col.1855.
33. See the chapter following.
34. Hansard, 1949 Vol.457, col.232.
35 Gwynn, *op.cit.* p.187.
36. PRO CAB/129/31.
37. *ibid.*
38. PRO CP(49)4.
39. PRO CAB/21/1842.
40. PRO CP(49)5.
41. PRO CP(49)47.
42. *ibid.*
43. PRO CAB/21/1842.
44. Bell, *op.cit.* p.43.
45. See the chapter following.

6. 'Against Every Decent Principle' pages 86-99

1. Lord Longford, *Peace by Ordeal*, London: 1935.
2. PRO CAB/21/1838; emphasis as in the original.
3. *ibid.*
4. PRO CAB/128/14.
5. Lyons, *op.cit.* p.553.
6. N. Mansergh, 'Problems of Imperial Policy 1931-9' in *Survey of Commonwealth Affairs*, 1952, p.329.
7. Lyons, *op.cit.* p.557.
8. Farrell, *op.cit.* p.184.
9. *ibid.* p.186.
10. *ibid.* p.187.
11. *ibid.* p.187.
12. Hansard, 1949 Vol.464, col.1856.
13. *ibid.* cols.1857-8.
14. *ibid.* cols.1883-4.
15. *ibid.* cols.1887-8.
16. Although this was not the only reason. See Farrell, *op.cit.* p.178.
17. Hansard, 1949 Vol.464, col.1928.
18. *ibid.* col.1930.
19. *ibid.* cols.1931-4.

20. *ibid*. col.1951.
21. *ibid*. cols.1952-4.
22. *Daily Herald*, 12 May 1949.
23. *Daily Worker*, 16 May 1949.
24. *Daily Herald*, 13 May 1949.
25. Hansard, 1949 Vol.465, col.48.
26. *ibid*. col.107.
27. *ibid*. cols.109-10.
28. *ibid*. col.113.
29. *Daily Worker*, 17 May 1949.
30. *Daily Worker*, 20 May 1949.
31. *Daily Herald*, 18 May 1949.
32. Hansard, 1949 Vol.465, cols.383-6.
33. *Daily Herald*, 13 May 1949.
34. *Daily Herald*, 20 May 1949.
35. PRO CAB/128/14.
36. Donoughue and Jones, *op.cit*. p.443.
37. *ibid*. p.308,
38. These and the following quotes are from the *Labour Party Conference Report*, 1949, p.133.

7. Inertia   pages 100-117

1. *Sunday Times*, 13 July 1980.
2. Terence O'Neill, *The Autobiography of Terence O'Neill*, London: Rupert Hart-Davis 1972, p.21.
3. *ibid*. p.62.
4. Sunday Times Insight Team, *Ulster*, London: Penguin, 1972, p.33.
5. See, for example: *Disturbances in Northern Ireland: Report of the Commission Appointed by the Government of Northern Ireland (Cameron Commission)*, Belfast: HMSO 1969; Michael Farrell, *Northern Ireland the Orange State*, London: Pluto Press 1976.
6. Harold Wilson, *The Labour Government, 1964-70*, London: Weidenfeld and Nicolson 1971, p.270.
7. Farrell, *op.cit*. p.242.
8. O'Neill, *op.cit*. p.83.
9. Wilson, *op.cit*. pp.670-1.
10. Paul Rose, *Backbencher's Dilemma*, London: Frederick Muller 1981, pp.195-6.
11. Sunday Times Insight Team, *op. cit*. p.80.
12. James Callaghan, *A House Divided*, London: Collins 1973.
13. Rose, *op. cit*. p.180.

14. Campaign of Democracy in Ulster papers in the Belfast Public Record Office.
15. Rose, *op.cit.* p.178.
16. *ibid.* p.179.
17. Wilson, *op.cit.* p.671.
18. *ibid.* p.672.
19. Callaghan, *op.cit.* p.10.
20. Wilson, *op.cit.* p.673.
21. Richard Crossman, *The Diaries of a Cabinet Minister*, Vol.3, 1968-70, London: Hamilton and Cape 1971, p.453.
22. *ibid.* p.458.
23. *Socialist Challenge*, 16 October 1980.
24. Crossman, *op.cit.* p.458.
25. *ibid.* p.483.
26. Callaghan, *op.cit.* p.15.
27. Crossman, *op.cit.* p.602.
28. Sunday Times Insight Team, *op.cit.* p.105.
29. *ibid.* p.103.
30. *ibid.* p.110.
31. *ibid.* p.142.
32. Callaghan, *op.cit.* p.137.
33. *ibid.* p.43.
34. Crossman, *op.cit.* p.619.
35. Crossman, *op.cit.* p.622.
36. Wilson, *op.cit.* p.692.
37. *ibid.* p.697.
38. O'Neill, *op.cit.* p.141.
39. *ibid.* pp.134-5.
40. Callaghan, *op.cit.* p.191.
41. *Labour Party Conference Report*, 1969, p.177.
42. *ibid.* p.171.
43. *ibid.* p.175.
44. *ibid.* p.184.
45. Callaghan, *op.cit.* p.87.
46. Eamonn McCann, *War and an Irish Town*, London: Penguin 1974, p.70.
47. Callaghan, *op.cit.* p.71.
48. *Labour Party Conference Report*, 1969, p.181.
49. *ibid.* p.182.
50. *ibid.* p.173.
51. *ibid.* p.184.
52. *Observer*, 26 November 1978.
53. Labour Party Conference Report, 1971, p.276.
54. *ibid.* p.276.

55. Sunday Times Insight Team, *op.cit*. p.213.
56. Callaghan, *op.cit*. p.146.
57. *ibid*. p.64.
58. *ibid*. p.178.
59. *Irish Times*, 3 April 1979.
60. Callaghan, *op.cit*. p.178.
61. *ibid*. p.178.
62. *ibid*. pp.165-7.
63. Hansard, 1971 Vol.823, cols.32-33.
64. *Labour Party Conference Report*, 1971, p.80.
65. *ibid*. pp.278-9.
66. Callaghan, *op.cit*. p.174.
67. Hansard, 1971 Vol.826, col.1572.
68. Hansard Vol.826, cols.1578-93.

8. Bipartisanship   pages 118-134

1. *Labour Party Conference Report*, 1972, p.384.
2. *ibid*. p.326.
3. Hansard 1972 Vol.835, cols.521-2.
4. Callaghan, *op.cit*. pp.156-7.
5. For the best account of the strike see, Robert Fisk, *The Point of No Return*, London: Andre Deutsch 1975.
6. *Irish Times*, 4 September 1974.
7. Rose, *op.cit*. p.183.
8. *Sunday Times*, 18 June 1978.
9. *Labour Party Conference Report*, 1974, p.293.
10. *ibid*. p.294.
11. *ibid*.
12. *ibid*.
13. *Sunday Times*, 18 June 1978.
14. *ibid*.
15. *Irish Times*, 13 September 1976.
16. Labour Party Research Department, 'Information Paper No 21', September 1976, p.1, in the Labour Party archives.
17. *ibid*. p.2.
18. *ibid*. p.4.
19. *ibid*. p.6.
20. *ibid*. p.11.
21. *ibid*. p.19.
22. *ibid*.
23. *ibid*. p.23.
24. *ibid*.
25. *The Times*, 18 December 1976.

26. *Irish Times*, 24 February 1977.
27. *Irish Times*, 14 November 1977.
28. *ibid.*
29. *Guardian*, 3 May 1978.
30. *Irish Times*, 7 May 1977.
31. *Irish Times*, 26 May 1977.
32. Peter Taylor, *Beating the Terrorists?*, London: Penguin 1980, p.78.
33. *The Times*, 24 February 1977.
34. *Irish Times*, 16 May 1979.
35. *Irish Times*, 30 December 1977.
36. *An Phoblacht*, 12 May 1979.
37. See Richard Harvey, *Diplock and the Assault on Civil Liberties*, London: Haldane Society, p.80; Kevin Boyle, Tom Hadden and Paddy Hillyard, *Ten Years on in Northern Ireland*, London: Cobden Trust 1980; Patricia Hewitt, *The Abuses of Power*, Oxford: Martin Robinson 1982.
38. Taylor, *op.cit.* p.229.
39. For more information on Prevention of Terrorism Act see, Peter Hain (ed.), Derek Humphry, Brian Rose-Smith, *Policing the Police*, Vol.I, London: John Calder 1979.
40. *ibid.* and Harvey, *op.cit.*
41. *Irish Times*, 12 January 1978.
42. *Observer*, 26 November 1978.
43. *Irish Times*, 19 November 1977.
44. *Daily Mail*, 6 January 1977; *Observer*, 23 January 1977.
45. *Irish Times*, 12 January 1978.
46. *Irish Times*, 11 March 1978.
47. *Irish Times*, 13 April 1978.
48. *Irish Times*, 2 November 1978.
49. *Irish Times*, 6 February 1979.
50. *ibid.*
51. *ibid.*
52. Barbara Castle, *The Castle Dairies*, London: Weidenfeld and Nicolson 1981, p.69, confirms that it was Callaghan who made the initiative.
53. *The Times*, 5 August 1974.
54. Hansard, 1974 Vol.871, cols.1421-2.
55. Hansard, 1976 Vol.907, col.1520.
56. Hansard, 1978 Vol.959, col.285.
57. *ibid.* cols.293-4.
58. *Irish Times* 16 March 1979.
59. *Daily Telegraph*, 18 January 1979.
60. Hansard, 1979 Vol.965, cols.520-2.

9. 'What about Ireland?'   pages 135-150

1. Hansard, 1979 Vol.965, col.516.
2. *Belfast Newsletter*, 4 May 1979.
3. *Daily Express*, 14 August 1979.
4. *Ireland Socialist Review*, No.6, Winter 1979-80, p.17.
5. *ibid*.
6. Labour Party News Release, 14 June 1980. (S110/80)
7. K. Coates, *What Went Wrong*, London: Spokesman 1979.
8. T. Benn, *Arguments for Socialism*, London: Jonathan Cape 1979.
9. This account of the conference is drawn from *Ireland Socialist Review*, No.6, Winter 1979-80.
10. For the entire speech see *Socialist Challenge*, 16 October 1980.
11. The full paper was not made public, but was supplied to the author by Reg Freeson, MP.
12. For a full record of opinion polls on Ireland see, *Voices For Withdrawal*, London: Committee for the Withdrawal from Ireland 1979.
13. Labour Party RD/556a/Dec 1980.
14. Labour Party Consultative Paper, January 1981.
15. Full test of speech supplied to the author by Kevin McNamara, MP.
16. Labour Party, RD/827/April 1981.
17. *ibid*.
18. Study Group minutes, 25 February 1981, Labour Party archives.
19. *ibid*. 25 March 1981.
20. *The Times*, 6 May 1981.
21. *Irish Times*, 9 April 1981.
22. *Irish Times*, 4 May 1981.
23. *Irish Times*, 13 May 1981.
24. *The Times*, 18 May 1981.
25. Hansard, 1981 Vol.7, No.133, cols.1047-8.
26. Labour Party National Executive Committee, *Statement on Northern Ireland to the 1981 Party Conference*, Labour Party, 1981, p.11.
27. *Socialist Challenge*, 8 October 1981.
28. For the views of the world's media see Counter Information Services, *Anti-Report 1981*.
29. *The Times*, 23 August 1981.
30. *ibid*.
31. Labour Committee on Ireland: *Labour and Ireland*, No.6.
32. Labour Party RD/827/April 1981.
33. Labour Party National Executive Committee, p.7.

Index